AMERICA 100 YEARS AGO
The beauty of old America illustrated

OLD FAITHFUL GEYSER IN ACTION.

(*From a photograph by Haynes, of St. Paul.*)

See page 218.

AMERICA
100 YEARS AGO
The beauty of old America illustrated

by

Richard Lovett, M.A.

EXCALIBUR BOOKS
NEW YORK

First published 1891
by the Religious Tract Society

This edition first published in the USA
1985 by Excalibur Books

Distributed by Bookthrift, Inc.
45 West 36th Street, New York, NY 10018

Excalibur is a trademark of Simon & Schuster Inc.
New York, New York

Bookthrift is a registered trademark of
Simon & Schuster Inc. New York, New York.
All rights reserved.

ISBN 0-671-80799-4

Printed and bound by R. J. Acford, Chichester,
England.

THE CUNARD STEAMSHIP UMBRIA.

INTRODUCTION.

FOR a number of years the 'Pen and Pencil Series' had upon its list a volume entitled *American Pictures*. It was written by the late Dr. Manning, and enjoyed a wide popularity. But in America things move quickly, and this book in almost all of its engravings, and in much of the letterpress, now possesses only an antiquarian value. Hence the resolution was taken to prepare an entirely new book; and to prevent all possibility of confusion with its predecessor, a new title was taken. *United States Pictures* has not a line of text in common with *American Pictures*, and of the one hundred and ninety-six engravings in the latter only five reappear in the former.

The author of the present volume has, he ventures to think, some special qualifications for the task he has undertaken. He spent nearly ten years of his youth in the United States, and he lived there all through the terrible struggle of the sanguinary Civil War between the Northern and Southern States from 1861 to 1865. He was educated at an American school, and came under the influence of many American habits of thought at a time when impressions once received abide for a lifetime. In the year 1890 he revisited the country after an absence of many years; travelling in almost every part, and comparing the impressions of mature manhood with the recollections of early life. This experience, while it has in no sense lessened his deep interest in the life of the United States, and his brotherly affection for the people, has impressed him with a firmer conviction than ever that the phenomena of United States life and government are of vital moment to the people of Great Britain, and should be most carefully noted by them at the present time. Trending we undoubtedly are in the direction along which the United States has travelled so far. Hence the way in which that great nation is working out the complicated and difficult questions of federal, state and municipal government; education; universal suffrage; the absolute equality of all religious beliefs in the eye of the law; protection versus free trade; currency; land transfer and tenure; and a host of other matters that come very close to the sources and springs of national prosperity, should be full of instruction for every thoughtful and observant man.

Some of these questions are touched, necessarily with a very light hand, in this book. If he has ventured to criticize in any respect the action of the United States in regard to any of them, he trusts that readers on that side of the water into whose hands the book may fall will believe that he has done so, not from any desire to find fault, but from the honest desire to enable his readers at home to gain the impressions produced upon his own mind by things as he saw them. England has many things to learn from her 'kin beyond the sea;' possibly the most important being *not* to attempt some great experiments they are trying, until the results of the great object lessons which the United States is giving to the world become a little clearer and more definite.

The charm of the United States to the lover of scenery consists in looking upon the natural wonders of that vast country as exemplified in the Hudson, Niagara, the great cañons of the West, the Yosemite, and the Yellowstone Park. To those more deeply concerned about social, political and commercial matters, it consists rather—at any rate so far as relates to the territory west of the Mississippi—in being able to watch a great nation actually in the process of making. Towns like Denver and Portland and Spokane Falls seem to grow almost beneath the eye of the visitor. The plan of this work has been to say comparatively little about the Eastern cities, and to give as much space as possible to the great and in many respects unique charms of the scenery. It is for this reason that both pen and pencil have dealt much more liberally with the Yosemite than with Chicago; and that the Grand Cañon of the Colorado is somewhat fully described, while towns like St. Louis, Cincinnati, and a host of others are not even mentioned. The books in the series to which this belongs never exceed 224 pages in length, and hence many departments one would have liked to treat have had to be wholly passed by.

In the selection of illustrations also there have been difficulties. The resources of the *Century, Scribner's Magazine,* and *Harper's Magazine* have been utilized. When a place or a thing had been well done in one or other of those publications, it seemed useless expense to re-engrave them.

But the book contains a large number of engravings done expressly for it by Mr. Edward Whymper, and these have been reserved, so far as possible,

TAKING THE PILOT ON BOARD OFF NEW YORK.

for subjects not treated at all before, or, if engraved, not executed in such a style as to make them worthy of a place.

A word or two must be said about the journey across the Atlantic, which is the inevitable prelude of a trip to the United States. The dread of this annually prevents many who would otherwise be very glad to set foot upon American soil from making the effort. This hindrance is more easily overcome by our American cousins, if we may judge by the increasing numbers who visit Europe every year. But, in reality, science as applied to steamship building, has made, and is still making, extraordinary improvements in the way of increasing the comfort of those who cross the ocean. The author made his last trip both out and home in the magnificent steamer, the Umbria, belonging to the old and famous Cunard Line. Notwithstanding the rivalry of younger and powerful competitors this line fully holds its own. The management is characterised now, as it ever has been, by care and skill; and it is a somewhat fastidious taste which requires or expects greater comfort or a faster pace across the Atlantic than is enjoyed by the passengers on the Umbria or the Etruria.

The author's end will be attained if by means of these pictures and descriptions some clear conception is given to the reader of the enormous size, the extraordinary natural beauties and advantages, the rapid growth, and the business opportunities of the United States. He would also be ungrateful indeed if he did not fully acknowledge the prompt and ready courtesy, and the large hospitality with which every native of 'the old home' is welcomed in all parts of the land over which wave the stars and the stripes. Every influence that helps to make England and the United States better known to each other is a blessing to both peoples; and this book is sent forth in the earnest hope that it may contribute in some measure to this great end.

THE TREASURY AT WASHINGTON.

CONTENTS AND LIST OF ILLUSTRATIONS.

—◦◦°⊙°◦◦—

CHAPTER I.

NEW YORK AND BROOKLYN.

CHAPTER I.—*continued.*

CHAPTER II.

NEW ENGLAND.

CHAPTER III.

THE CRADLE OF INDEPENDENCE.

CHAPTER IV.

THE FEDERAL CAPITAL.

CHAPTER V.

THE SOUTH.

CHAPTER VI.

TO CHICAGO VIÂ NIAGARA.

CHAPTER VII.

TO SAN FRANCISCO VIÂ DENVER AND SALT LAKE CITY.

CHAPTER VIII.

THE PACIFIC COAST AND THE YOSEMITE VALLEY.

CHAPTER IX.

FROM PORTLAND TO THE YELLOWSTONE PARK.

MOUNT SHASTA.

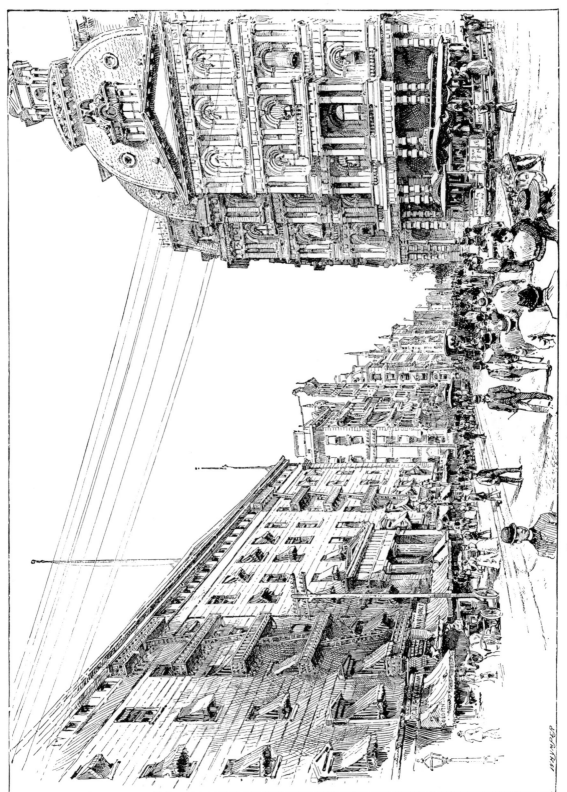

BROADWAY, SHOWING ASTOR HOUSE AND THE POST OFFICE.

THE NARROWS, NEW YORK HARBOUR.

CHAPTER I.

NEW YORK AND BROOKLYN.

THE ELEVATED RAILWAY.

THE great majority of Europeans who visit the United States enter that vast country through the port of New York. And if the entrance be made in daylight, and the sky is sunny and serene, their first impressions of the New World are likely to be most favourable. The eye that for six or seven days has had to content itself with the somewhat limited range of colour afforded by the blue and gray and white of the Atlantic in calm and storm, and the wider though still limited range of colouring afforded by an ocean sky, feasts with delight upon the soft hues of the New Jersey hills, and upon the lovely islets and wooded slopes of New York Harbour. The great steamer slowly and with dignity makes her way along the winding channel and through the Narrows, amid the fleet of varied shipping, and past the lofty statue of Liberty, until at length the commercial capital of the Republic lies before her.

Occupying the whole of Manhattan Island, and overflowing into all the surrounding districts, New York is shaped like an irregular V, and is bounded on the west by the Hudson, and on the east by the East River. On every hand signs of life and industry abound. Saucy little tugs puff

Customs' Officers Examining Baggage on a Steamer's Wharf at New York.

noisily about the lovely bay.   Scores and scores of vessels, from the great
ocean liner down to the tiny sloop, crowd the wide waterways.
Numerous lines of large steam ferryboats cross the river and the harbour
in every direction, and as the new-comer looks with eager interest upon the
city he is at once impressed with three things : the dense masses of shipping
that crowd the wharves, the enormous piles of building that uprear themselves
into the sky, as though bent upon realising the never-completed purpose of
the builders of the original Tower of Babel, and the great bridge so
skilfully thrown across the broad East River at such a height that the
masts of the largest vessels pass easily beneath it.

There are no docks of the kind so common at Liverpool and London.
All the shipping, from the small barges up to the steamer of 10,000 tons,
discharges and takes on board cargo and passengers from wharves that jut
out into the Hudson and East Rivers.   And no sooner has the great vessel
been safely moored to the wharf than the ordeal of the Custom House has
to be encountered.   So far as the consumption of time goes, the writer's
experience is that the Custom House at New York is less troublesome than
at Liverpool.   But since in England the list of dutiable articles contains
about twelve items, while in the United States it is about twelve hundred,
the search at New York is not unfrequently an exasperating and troublesome
experience.   Until the inspector has chalked certain hieroglyphics upon each
article of his baggage, the traveller must bear this infliction as best he can ;
but as soon as this is done, he is at liberty to take himself and his
belongings whithersoever he desires.

And here, again, he meets with unfamiliar customs.   At the shore end
of the quay stand a crowd of men all eager to convey him and his baggage
away.   But ere he takes a seat in one of these carriages, and entrusts his
property to the driver, he had better conclude an exact bargain with that
gentleman.   He will be surprised to learn that the shortest journey will
cost him as much as the longest cab drive within the four-mile radius of
London ; that although there is a fixed tariff, it is rarely or never heeded ;
and that if he goes about much in these four-wheeled vehicles their hire
will form a very large item of expenditure.   A dollar (four shillings) a mile
is a not infrequent charge, the legal rate being just half that sum.   If
unwilling or unable to afford cabs of this kind, what is the traveller to do?
He can avail himself at once of the express system.   Great companies exist
for the purpose of conveying not only all articles of commerce, but also
personal baggage, safely, expeditiously, and on the whole very cheaply, to
all parts of the United States.   The traveller, if he wishes, can on the
landing wharf at New York express his trunk to San Francisco, and have
no further trouble with it until he requires it in that distant town.   Or he
can entrust it to the proper agent, take a receipt for it, and an hour or two
after he has reached his hotel or residence, his one, two, or twenty trunks,

as the case may be, will be safely delivered at the address he has given.
A still more economical method, and one escaping the somewhat high charges
of the express system, is to 'check' all the heavy baggage, that is, deposit
it in the baggage-room at the station, receiving in return a numbered brass
check for each article. The baggage then goes free of charge to the
station to which it is checked, and it is kept safely and only given up on

THE BAGGAGE-ROOM AT A RAILWAY-STATION.

presentation of the proper checks. If kept at any station for more than
twenty-four hours a trifling charge for storage is made. So well understood
is this system, and so universal, that almost all travellers in the United
States carry in a handbag such articles as they require for immediate use,
and 'check' from place to place all their weighty baggage.

The great steamship companies land their passengers in the immediate neighbourhood of the Cunard Company, Pier No. 39, North River, as the Hudson is commonly called near its mouth, or on the Jersey shore opposite. Hence the first view of New York streets is by no means the most attractive. Riverside districts in great ports are rarely either savoury or pleasing to the eye, and New York is no exception to this rule. But at once the new arrival can begin to appreciate the unusual facilities for locomotion which abound in all American cities. Several lines of tram cars run along West Street, the thoroughfare that skirts the Hudson, and these connect with others that reach the most remote parts. At a distance of only two 'blocks'—the term used almost everywhere in the United States to describe the distance between two parallel streets—runs the Ninth Avenue branch of the Elevated Railway, and by this means of transit almost any district of the city can be rapidly reached. Many of the hotels are within walking distance of the landing-piers, and if the arrival falls within the hours of daylight, few things are more interesting than a first walk along the streets of New York.

The southern end of Manhattan Island is the site of what may be termed ancient New York. It was here that the original tiny Dutch settlement stood; here the streets are irregular, and have names possessing some amount of local and historical interest; and here is centred the great mass of financial and mercantile business, which enables New York to rank next to London among the commercial centres of the world. In London the ancient landmarks have been largely swept away by the flood of modern building; in New York, though the oldest were only contemporary with Temple Bar, they have almost entirely disappeared. The life of New York, as known to the civilised world, begins with that notable voyage made in the Half-Moon by Henry Hudson, who, engaged by the Dutch East India Company for the impossible task of finding a northern passage to China, skirted a large part of the eastern coast of the continent, and on September 3, 1609, entered the harbour now so well known as New York Bay, sailed up the magnificent river ever since known by his name as far as the present State capital, Albany, and by right of discovery claimed the land for Holland. Towards the close of 1614, a Dutch colony arrived, and built a fort and four houses upon what is now known as Bowling Green.

The little settlement was originally called New Amsterdam, and grew slowly but steadily. In 1648 it numbered 1,000 inhabitants; in 1684, by its surrender to the British under the Duke of York, it changed both its nationality and name, and has ever since been known as New York. In 1700 its population was 6,000. At the close of the struggle for independence it began to grow rapidly both in numbers and importance. In 1800 it had increased to 60,489, in 1850 to 515,847, in 1880 to 1,206,590, and in 1890 to 1,513,501.

Few great cities are so easy to master topographically as New York. Comparatively narrow, and in the northern section laid out with mathematical regularity, a quarter of an hour spent in the careful study of a good map will enable anyone to fix permanently in his mind the leading thoroughfares and districts. In our brief survey of the most noteworthy regions and buildings, we cannot do better than follow the path marked out by the city's history. The little fort and four houses on Bowling Green of 1614 have expanded steadily in a northerly direction, and the city limits now reach nearly to Yonkers.

The southern extremity of Manhattan Island is preserved as a public park, and in its name, the Battery, still commemorates the existence of the old Dutch fort. It is now wholly given over to the pursuits of peace, and affords a fine point of view from which to study the inner reaches of the bay and the busy shipping of the great port. On the western side stands the world-famous Castle Garden, the gate through which the vast tide of immigration has poured into the United States during the last fifty years. The gigantic scale of this immigration may be judged by a few figures. Between the years 1855 and 1882, no less than 7,892,783 immigrants reached the United States, and of these 5,169,765 passed through New York. In one year, 1882, no less than 476,086, that is, over 9,000 per week, landed here. For many years these and similar facts were a source of gratification and even pride to the citizens of the great Republic. It was maintained—and we are far from saying that facts do not largely sustain the contention—that in the vast regions under Federal control, the enormous numbers who in Ireland, and England, and Germany, and other European countries, seemed doomed to lives of perpetual struggle and poverty, could find happy homes and a comfortable livelihood. Myriads have put the contention to the proof, and much of the brain, and nerve, and muscle of the Republic have come from the older lands of the East. But the United States are beginning to find that this incoming flood is not an unmixed blessing. As population increases, social problems of the kind that trouble the older civilisations, though their manifestations may not take exactly the same form, make themselves and their difficulties felt. The native-born American begins to think that there are worse evils than a sparsely populated country, and hence the English traveller meets with enactments like the Contract Labour and the Pauper Emigrant statutes, which at first sight appear to be a flat contradiction to the boast that the United States opens wide her doors to all and any who will come, and there find a home. By the Contract Labour statute it is declared illegal for any man or any company of men to enter the United States, if their arrival is due to any engagement on their part to work for, or to carry out, any labour contract with men already resident in the United States. It is in fact a boycott enforced by the great labour organisations. Labour difficulties are not

IMMIGRANTS AT NEW YORK.

unknown in the States, and the labour vote is so powerful that, in order to conciliate it, Congress passed this law. The result is that, in great strikes, the superfluous working populations of Europe cannot be used openly to replace the men who have gone out. To say that the law is not evaded would be absurd. Men are told that work is to be had in certain districts, and they go to these districts and find it. It is all accidental, of course, in the eye of the law; but it happens sometimes, even in the face of the Contract Labour statute, that Italians and men of other European nationalities appear in considerable numbers in those parts of the States where labour troubles exist, although it cannot be proved that anyone asked them to come there.

The Pauper Emigrant statute has quite another object in view. The Republic is usually ready to welcome and to employ skilled labour of any kind. But it begins in many centres of population to find that immigration has drawbacks peculiar to itself. It is only natural that among the millions of immigrants who have poured into the States there should have been a considerable percentage of the idle, vicious and useless—except for mischief. By the statute referred to, power is bestowed upon the United States officials at New York and other ports of entry to prohibit from landing, and to compel the return whence they came, any intending immigrants who cannot satisfactorily demonstrate that they have a reasonable prospect of being able to earn a respectable livelihood. This law has been passed mainly to conciliate the labour interest, but it is also viewed favourably by many who feel that the presence of an ignorant, poverty-stricken and not improbably vicious element of this class, is certainly a drag on the national prosperity, and may even become a positive danger. But while it is hardly possible for the intelligent observer to withhold a certain measure of sympathy from the objects of these statutes, it is equally impossible to avoid the feeling that they somewhat discount the value of the boast so often made, and in the past so well attested, that the great Republic threw open wide her hospitable doors to the downtrodden and the needy of all nationalities.

Starting at the Battery, and bisecting Manhattan Island through its whole length of twelve and a half miles, runs the great thoroughfare of New York, Broadway. This is a handsome, wide street, enriched along the first seven miles with very fine buildings, consisting almost entirely of business houses, hotels, public offices, and structures of the various kinds which cluster in the main street of a great commercial metropolis. Many of them possess architectural pretensions of no mean order, handsome façades of white marble and different kinds of stone being very numerous. Our purpose of gaining a birdseye view of New York can hardly be better accomplished than by a stroll along Broadway, with an occasional excursion to interesting localities to the east or to the west of that great business artery. In his first walk along Broadway the visitor will be struck, as he was in the sail up the bay, with the advertising enterprise displayed on every hand. The fronts of the buildings are covered with signs, which for boldness of effect, variety of design, and minuteness of detail in describing the wares and functions of the proprietors, are quite unrivalled in any European city. The ceaseless stream of tram cars, which by their diverse colours and route-signs evidently penetrate to all parts of the city, again impresses him with the importance attached to easy locomotion. The way in which the thoroughfare is cut up by the lines would scandalise such an advanced body even as the London County Council, but in New York is accepted as a matter of course. In the numerous vehicles through which he threads his way in crossing the broad street he sees unfamiliar objects. Many of the vehicles intended for the carriage of heavy articles are built on very different plans from those common in Europe, and there is also an unfamiliar lightness about many of the vehicles used for driving purposes.

TRINITY CHURCH.

But his walk will not have extended from Bowling Green to the first object of special interest in his 'up-town' journey, Trinity Church, ere he finds himself pondering two problems : first, how it comes about that Broadway is so badly paved, and secondly, why the residents and business men tolerate such a state of things. If he glances at the side streets he notices that as a rule they are much worse than the main thoroughfare. If he pushes inquiries on this subject he will soon find that it branches out into an investigation not altogether creditable to the public spirit of the Empire City. 'Why,' said the writer to a young New York lawyer, 'are your streets so much worse paved than ours in London?' 'Well,' he replied, 'it's not because we do not spend as much money upon them. We do ; but most of the money stops before it gets to the street.' Closer inspection of New York habits, and more intimate acquaintance with its life, confirms the truth of this remark in relation to other departments besides that of paving. In New York two aspects of life in the United States may be studied to great advantage. The first is, the unrivalled commercial enterprise and 'go' there shown. Fortunes have been made with unexampled rapidity in New York, and while the centre for this kind of success has now shifted to the west of the Mississippi, New York still remains the happy hunting-ground of the railroad man, the financier, and the great merchant. But so concentrated has been the general attention upon business, so engrossing have been its demands, that in their great haste to become rich the dwellers in New York seem to have taken little or no pains to develop a healthy public spirit, to secure anything approaching probity in municipal life, and to maintain adequate control over the expenditure of public money. The result might have been anticipated. A large percentage of the scum of immigration settles in New York. Universal suffrage puts great political power into the hands of large numbers of men who are absolutely unfit to use it except for selfish and corrupt purposes, and hence New York is an object lesson in two very important respects.

It is distinctly bad for a city to be so given up to commercial pursuits that it cannot even take time and trouble to rescue its municipal government from the control of men who persistently put personal and private ends before the public weal. It is a calamity for a city like New York to so arrange its municipal government that it shall be possible for men like the late Boss Tweed and the present Tammany Hall ring, not only to influence but even to absolutely control civic affairs, and to do this in such a way as to enrich themselves while they disgracefully neglect civic responsibilities. The past scandals connected with the enlargement of the City Hall, and the present condition of New York streets, which are a reproach to any self-respecting community, are alike commentaries not altogether favourable upon the question whether the widest suffrage is an unrestricted blessing to the community.

Trinity Church, already referred to, is one of the landmarks of New York. The tall spire, towering up to a height of 284 feet, is a fine point of view from which to study the topography of New York. The church itself is a handsome structure of brown stone, built in the Gothic style, and richly decorated with stained glass. It contains the very splendid Astor Memorial Reredos, erected in 1878. The parish is the oldest in the city, and the first church dated from 1696. The present building was begun in 1839, and completed in 1846. Directly facing Trinity Church, and running at right angles to Broadway, is Wall Street, the great financial centre of New York and the United States. It runs from the central thoroughfare to the East River, and from the foot of it one of the numerous ferries to Brooklyn starts. It contains some very fine buildings, the chief of which are—the United States Sub-Treasury, a fine

From Harper's Magazine.

WALL STREET.

Copyright, by Harper & Brothers.

white marble building in the Doric style, 200 feet long and 80 feet wide, standing on the site of the old Federal Hall in which George Washington delivered his first address as President of the United States; the U. S. Custom House, built of Quincy granite, formerly the Exchange, an imposing and massive erection of the old style; the Drexel Building, and many magnificent modern banks and financial offices. The Stock Exchange is in Broad Street, only a few steps from Wall Street, and its members, unlike their brethren of the London Stock Exchange, are courteous enough to admit the public into galleries overlooking the floor of the house. Here in times of financial disturbance scenes of the wildest excitement occur, and even on quiet days, if a blind man were brought in and asked to judge from the sounds which fill the building the character of the occupants, he might easily be forgiven for thinking that he was in a menagerie full of hungry beasts.

Returning to Broadway and pursuing our course northwards, we soon reach one of the busiest spots in New York, the corner of Fulton Street, so named after the famous steamboat inventor. Just beyond Fulton Street is a wide open space, shown in the illustration on page 14, formed by the junction of Broadway and Park Row, which here makes an acute angle with the great street. In the angle formed by Park Row and Broadway formerly stood a fine open park in the shape of a triangle, called City Hall Park. But at the close of the Civil War part of this ground was set apart for the new Post Office, a very handsome granite building of four storeys, having façades on Broadway and Park Row each over 260 feet long, and a frontage towards the Park of 279 feet, with a lofty Mansard roof. The building, which cost about £1,250,000, is fireproof, and the upper floors are used by the United States Courts.

In the rear of the Post Office, and nearly in the centre of the Park, stands the City Hall, a three-storey building in the Italian style, faced in front and at the sides with white marble. Here is the seat of the municipal government. At the north end stands the new Court House, which, though begun in 1861 and occupied since 1867, was not completed until about 1885. In connection with this building the notorious 'Ring Frauds' took place, the bill for the structure and furniture amounting to over £2,400,000. Although Tweed and his associates suffered in the long run the penalty of their crimes, and the tale of their gigantic robberies has long been ancient history, yet it may not be out of place to refer here briefly to the ugly story, since it illustrates the most serious danger to which large cities in the United States are exposed. Even at the present time (1891) the municipality of New York is not free from men who are quite as willing as Tweed was to enrich themselves at the public expense. In the great upheaval that followed the exposure of 1871, men of this type lost for a season their preponderating influence. But, the first force of the reaction spent, they began to renew their old practices, and the bulk of the citizens, too absorbed in commercial and other private enterprises, allowed matters to fall back into something like the old state of corruption. Tweed was a typical 'boss,' that is, a man skilful enough to so marshal and control all the worst element in the municipal voters as to be able to direct not only the whole city government, but, whenever necessary, the State government also.

Tweed began life as a fireman in one of the old volunteer companies, and soon rose to the post of foreman. All who remember how popular these companies were with the New York rabble prior to 1860, can easily understand the power he thus gained. In 1850 he was elected alderman, and in 1853 was sent to Congress. He soon perceived that New York

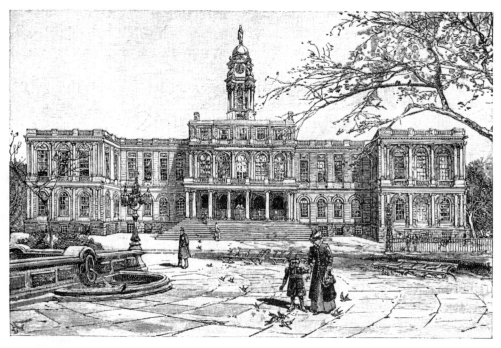

THE NEW YORK CITY HALL.

offered a field for the exercise of his peculiar gifts, far more promising than Washington, and hence he secured for himself the post of President of the Board of Supervisors. This body had been created by the new city charter of 1857, and was the object of Tweed's solicitude, because it possessed the power to levy the local taxes and managed the county property and buildings. Hence it afforded unrivalled opportunities to the manipulator who was astute enough to divert its operations from the public good to his own private advantage. Tweed deemed it needful for his ends to secure the votes of the hosts of immigrants—for the most part the residuum—who stayed to swell the population of New York. In 1863 he obtained control of Tammany Hall, the supreme organisation of the Democratic party. By the simple but efficacious means of filling all public offices with their creatures, Tweed and his associates gradually secured all the chief posts in the city government, and enrolled under their banner a host bound to themselves by the powerful ties of self-interest. By frauds of the most unblushing nature, such, for example, as false registrations, unfair counting, and a free application on the day of election of the 'vote early and vote often' principle, they elected the mayor of New York, and finally the Governor of the State.

In this connection it is amusing to learn that a minor reform, consisting of the substitution of glass for wooden ballot boxes, has been very unpopular with Tweed's successors, for the simple reason that it curtails somewhat the pleasant practice of inserting a considerable number of ballot papers *before the election begins!* So well had Tweed's policy succeeded that, in 1869, all departments of the city government were completely in the hands of himself or of his nominees. Emboldened by success, the conspirators proceeded to reform the civic government, abolished the old Board of Supervisors, greatly increased the power of the mayor, and placed the absolute control of all civic expenditure in the hands of a Board of Apportionment, composed of Tweed and three other men upon whom he could rely. Having thus secured the control of the essential offices, the other appointments were filled by the mayor with men, many of whose names carried credit and weight; they thus being skilfully used to allay any suspicions that might have been aroused by the new departure.

By a still freer use of means already described this Board secured, during the year 1871, control of civic funds to the amount of £9,600,000. Rich beyond its wildest dreams, apparently omnipotent in the Empire State, the Ring aimed at even controlling the election of the President of the United States. But Boss Tweed found, as even the most successful scoundrels do generally find, that the time of his most conspicuous success was his time of greatest danger. All seemed to be going well. To carry out plunder connected with the widening of Broadway they bought over one of the city judges. On the new Court House, for which they were authorised to spend £50,000, they laid out £1,600,000. Tweed was even skilful enough to induce a committee of representative citizens to approve his policy, and to affirm that the city accounts were 'administered in a correct and faithful manner.'

But, on the large scale no less than on the small, thieves fall out and honest men get their rights. A clerk who received an appointment in the auditor's office by the influence of a man named O'Brien, who was not connected with Tammany Hall, happened to notice one day an account of enormous magnitude for plastering and furnishing the new Court House. Aware of the system then in vogue, and thinking it might be useful to his patron, he copied the account and sent his copy to O'Brien. The latter, having this important document in hand, naturally enough tried to use it for his own financial benefit. Failing in this object, he placed it at the disposal of the *New York Times*, and on July 8, 1871, that paper began the series of attacks which led to the ruin of the Ring. Excitement rose to a high pitch, and as a last resource Tweed resolved to throw over an old and trusted comrade. But the latter, finding himself deserted in this scandalous fashion, went over to the enemy, revealed all the secrets and methods of the Ring, and a great civic upheaval took place, and in the autumn of 1871 all the reform candidates were elected. All the members of the Ring paid the penalty in one form or other for their misdeeds, and Tweed finally died in prison. The financial loss inflicted by their mal-practices may be estimated from the fact that the city debt, which stood in 1860 at £4,000,000, had in 1871 risen to £21,000,000.

Just to the east of the City Hall Park stands Franklin Square, the centre of New York newspaper enterprise. Within a short distance of each other, in some cases almost side by side, stand the offices of the *Herald, Times, World*, and *Tribune*. Their rivalry has extended even into the realm of architecture. About 1866 the *Herald* built a splendid white marble office on the site formerly occupied by Barnum's Museum, an institution which used to delight juvenile New York a generation ago. In 1874 the *Tribune* put up a lofty pile, ten storeys high, and above the main building rises a clock tower to the height of 285 feet. The *Times*, not to be outdone by its neighbour and rival, also rebuilt its office, completing the work in 1890. This was done by skilfully adapting and enlarging the old building, which was a substantial fire-proof, six-storey structure. The architect propped up the outer parts of the floors, and then razed to the ground the outer walls on the three sides which face upon different streets, and upon their foundations built the new massive walls, and raised the whole edifice from six to thirteen storeys. This rebuilding was completed in fifteen months, *and during the whole time* the paper was printed and published on the premises! And finally the *World*, in 1890, put up a veritable Tower of Babel fourteen storeys high, with a tower containing six more floors, and crowned by a cupola, on the top of which is a lantern which can be seen from almost any part of the city, and which is 309 feet above the pavement of the street below. The press of the United States is managed with very great ability, possesses very large financial resources, and is manned by a staff whose energy and enterprise appear to be inexhaustible. But at the same time it exhibits many features which from an English point of view are most objectionable. This remark applies even to the great New York dailies whose home we have just visited. These are often occupied with descriptions of social incidents, public matters or private scandals given with a minuteness of personal detail and a warmth of colouring nearly, if not quite, unknown to the European press. Sunday journalism is also on the increase, all the great papers publishing Sunday issues. These often contain a wealth of varied, useful, and interesting information. Some of them are marvels of production. The *Chicago Tribune,*

for example, issues a Sunday number which extends to thirty-two pages. But, on the whole, the impression they make is that their influence is demoralising. Many of the Sunday issues are full of unsavoury police news, sporting intelligence, and social gossip. The English press is not perfection, and in many respects cannot afford to throw stones at its neighbours; but we trust that every attempt made to imitate the American press in its Sunday issues will result in complete failure.

Beyond the City Hall we pass a constant succession of splendid buildings, warehouses, offices, hotels, theatres, &c. At Astor Place we reach the district known as 'up town,' we enter upon one of the great literary and philanthropic districts of the city, and also reach the point where the old and irregular arrangement of streets gives way to the severely modern and rectangular method. Leaving Broadway for a moment, and passing through Astor Place, we find within a stone's throw four very important buildings: the Mercantile Library, con-

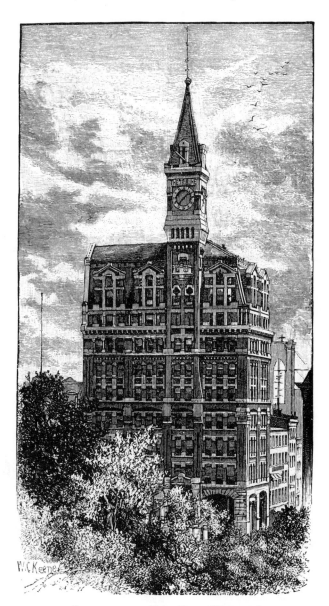

OFFICE OF THE NEW YORK 'TRIBUNE.'

taining over 200,000 volumes and a good reading-room; and the Astor Library, founded by John Jacob Astor, and richly endowed by him and his son, William B. Astor. The library contains a quarter of a million volumes, many of them of the highest rarity and excellence, and is complete in several special departments of study. It is open daily, and is for the free use of the public.   Hard by stands the spacious building known as the

A MEMBER OF THE 'BROADWAY SQUAD' ON DUTY.

Cooper Institute, founded and endowed by Peter Cooper, a wealthy New York merchant.   It has long been used for educational purposes, most of the noted men of modern times have spoken and lectured here, and it also contains a large library. Directly opposite stands the large six-storey brick building known as the Bible House, the home of the American Bible Society.

A New York Mansion.

Returning to Broadway, and pursuing our northward journey, we are struck by the handsome front of Grace Church which seems to jut out into the centre of the roadway, from the fact that Broadway here bends towards the left. A short stroll through one of the best shopping districts of New York brings us to Union Square, $3\frac{1}{2}$ acres in extent, surrounded

D

by very fine shops and hotels, including the famous jewellers, Tiffany & Co. The traffic of all kinds is very considerable, and along the whole extent of the great thoroughfare the services of the 'Broadway Squad'—that is, stalwart policemen whose duty it is to pilot pedestrians across—are in constant request. From this point Broadway runs north, through Madison Square, and on for another two miles until it reaches Central Park, at 59th Street. As already noted, at Astor Place the method of laying out New York alters. The streets which run north and south are known as Avenues, and beginning at the East River side are numbered First, Second, &c., up

THE BELVEDERE, CENTRAL PARK, NEW YORK.

to Twelfth, Lexington Avenue coming between Third and Fourth, and Madison Avenue between Fourth and Fifth. These Avenues are crossed at right angles by the streets, which all run due east and west, and beginning on the east at East 1st Street, and on the west at West 3rd Street, run up to 200-and-something Street. Fifth Avenue is the dividing line between east and west. As there are, on the average, twenty blocks or streets to the mile, if the visitor is at 10th Street, and wishes to go to 100th Street, he knows at once that he has about five miles to go. Loco-motion is easy and rapid by means of the Elevated Railway, which runs along Second, Third, Sixth and Ninth Avenues, intervening points being easily reached by trams or by walking. Probably no large city in the world is so easily traversed or so quickly made familiar to strangers as New York. Fifth Avenue, which begins at Washington Square and runs up the eastern side of Central Park, has long been noted as the fashionable centre of the New York residential portion. Many of the most splendid private edifices of the city are situated here, and in no quarter are to be seen more evidences of wealth and luxury. Some of the public buildings, especially the Fifth Avenue Hotel and St. Patrick's Cathedral (Roman Catholic) are very handsome, the latter being the finest specimen of church architecture in the city.

Central Park occupies a parallelogram in the centre of the 'up-town' district, about $2\frac{1}{2}$ miles long, and about half a mile wide. It is very well laid out, contains a good deal of water, and many fine walks and drives. The companion obelisk to Cleopatra's Needle stands near the centre of the Park. Fronting the Park, on Fifth Avenue and 70th Street, stands the Lenox Library, and directly behind it the Lenox Hospital, both the munificent bequest of the late James Lenox, one of the numerous American millionaires. The library contains an extraordinary number of the most precious books, and is especially rich in Americana, Tindale Testaments and early English Bibles, together with probably the most complete collections in the world of Milton and John Bunyan.

In addition to Central Park, New York has lately been enriched by the appropriation to public use of a large tract of the best situated land in Manhattan Island. The Hudson River forms a superb natural feature in the neighbourhood of New York. Its banks are utilised, as we have seen, for commercial and especially for shipping purposes, along the two or three miles ere it empties into New York Bay. But the whole space along its eastern shore, from 72nd to 130th Street, that is, for a distance of over three miles, is devoted to Riverside Park. While the Park was being roughly laid out General Grant died, and finally this site was chosen for his last resting-place. His mausoleum stands at the northern end of the Park, known as Claremont. The view at this point across the wide river, with the hills on the distant Jersey shore, just beginning to form the precipitous rocky walls known as the Palisades, the chief beauty of the Lower Hudson, is most attractive.

New York, in addition to its admirable public school system for primary education, possesses three large institutions for higher education —the College of the City of New York, the New York University, and

VIEW ACROSS THE HUDSON AT RIVERSIDE PARK.

Columbia College. To the first of these any lad of sufficient ability can pass from the public schools, equivalent to English Board Schools, and receive a University training entirely free of expense as regards tuition fees and college expenses. The New York University was founded in 1831, has a staff of fifty professors, and is attended by about five hundred students. The departments of arts and science and the law school of the New York University are housed in a very handsome marble building, situated in Washington Square; and there is a flourishing medical school in another part of the city.

Columbia College is the oldest educational institution in the State of New York, the charter dating from 1754. It is now one of the wealthiest in the Republic, possessing property in real estate estimated to be worth £1,000,000. It was originally called King's College, but upon its reconstruction after the Revolution, in 1784, the name was altered to Columbia College. In 1787 the idea of making it 'the mother of a University' originated, but the working of it out has occupied a century. The first President under the new scheme was William Samuel Johnson, a graduate of Yale, a friend of Dr. Johnson, a man of affairs, who held the office from 1787 to 1800. In his day, John Randolph was for a time a student. Since that day many men of high note in the United States, and some of a wider fame, have been connected with its staff. From 1820 to 1867 Charles Anthon held one or other of the classical chairs. In recent years the authorities of Columbia College have exhibited great activity. When it became needful to remove the College to its present site—the block bounded respectively by Madison and Fourth Avenues, and by 49th and 50th Streets—the opportunity was seized to re-organize the college, and to rebuild in greatly improved style the various schools and college structures. It now consists of Schools of Arts, Mines, Law,

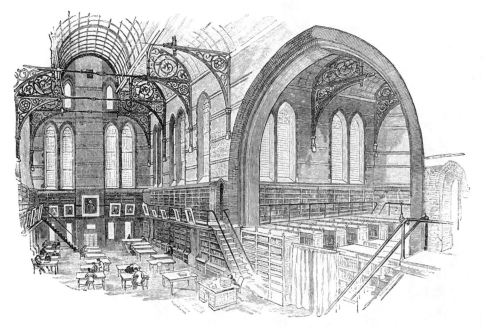

COLUMBIA COLLEGE—INTERIOR OF THE LIBRARY.

Political Science and Medicine, and as an adjunct a School of Library Economy, for the training of librarians. Including the Medical School, which is situated in 23rd Street, the college contains from 1,500 to 2,000 students, is practically a great University, and now, better than ever in the past, accomplishes the object emphasised by the committee report of 1810, that 'the primary principle of all sound education' is 'the evolution of faculty and the formation of habit.'

The reconstructed college buildings form a conspicuous addition to the new architecture of the city. The library is a very handsome structure, and the great collection of books is available from 8 A.M. to 10 P.M., not only to the students and graduates of the college, but to any who can show a good reason for the wish to consult any of its treasures.

Before bringing our rambles about New York to a close, we must make an excursion to the 'City of Churches,' as Brooklyn is called, from the number of spires visible in that district as the steamer sails up the Bay. Brooklyn is a distinct city in point of municipal arrangements, but it is practically as much a part of New York as Southwark is of London. It is a fact that the East River, a stream varying from half a mile to a mile and a half in width, rolls between New York and Brooklyn, but the magnificent suspension bridge, completed in 1883, which is still the largest structure of its kind in the world, has spanned this waterway. It is by this structure

COLUMBIA COLLEGE.

we will cross. The starting-point in New York is in Park Row, hard by the City Hall and Franklin Square. From this point to the corresponding end in Brooklyn is a distance of 5,989 feet. We can choose our method of traversing it. Every two or three minutes trains drawn by cable power cross, occupying five or six minutes on the journey; we can also drive across, if we are in an indolent mood. But, given a fine day free from wind, much the best plan is to walk. By this means we see the bridge to perfection, we get superb views over both cities, and also up the East River in the direction of Long Island Sound, and down the stream and away over the bay in the direction of the Narrows, Coney Island, and the wide waters of the Atlantic. Though mooted before, the scheme was greatly aided in its passage through the Legislature by the inconvenience caused to the ferry-boats by the ice in the winter of 1866–67. The writer well remembers the scenes of almost Arctic excitement and adventure for which that winter was famous. A charter was granted to a company, the capital was fixed at £1,000,000, with power to increase, New York and Brooklyn were to subscribe as their Common Councils saw fit. It was finally felt to be too great a matter to leave in the hands of any company, and so the original subscribers were paid off, and now New York owns two-thirds, and Brooklyn one-third of the undertaking. The engineer was John A. Roebling ; but he died in 1869, and the work was brought to a successful issue by his son, Washington A. Roebling. The foundation for the Brooklyn Tower was begun January 3, 1870. Thirteen years were occupied in the construction, the amount expended was £3,000,000, and it was opened for traffic on May 24, 1883.

The bridge is supported by two towers, which rise $276\frac{2}{3}$ feet above high-water mark. From these the bridge is swung so that its centre is 135 feet above high water, thus allowing ships of the largest tonnage to pass easily beneath. The river is crossed by this one span, which is $1,595\frac{1}{2}$ feet long. The graceful appearance is heightened by the fact that the bridge is gently curved, being 15 feet higher at the centre of the span than at the towers, and 46 feet higher than at the anchorages. The great cables pass over the towers, upon which they exert mainly a vertical pressure, and

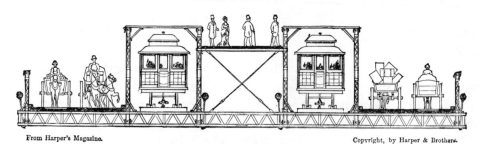

From Harper's Magazine.   Copyright, by Harper & Brothers.

SECTION OF THE BROOKLYN BRIDGE.

930 feet back from them pass into the anchorages. These are masses of solid masonry 132 feet by 119 feet at the base, which rise 90 feet above high-water mark, and contain in each case, there being one on each shore, 60,000 tons weight of material. We have no space to explain how rigidity, power to resist the wind, and freedom from oscillation have been imparted to this gigantic structure. It is as remarkable for its graceful lines as for utility, and now forms the most striking public work in New York, if not in the United States. The total weight of the whole central span is 6,740 tons, and it has been calculated that when most crowded with vehicles, foot-passengers, and cable-cars crammed to overflowing, as they usually are both morning and evening, the maximum weight it has to carry is 1,380 tons. The maximum strain of weight that can come upon the cables is about 12,000 tons, and they are of an ultimate strength of nearly 50,000 tons.

The steel framework of the bridge is portioned out into five parallel avenues, with an average width of 16 feet, separated from each other by vertical lines of strong steel truss-work. The outside avenues are each 19 feet wide, and are reserved for vehicles. Parallel with each of these, and on the inner side, run the two lines of cable-cars. The central avenue, which is reserved for foot-passengers, is 15½ feet wide, and is raised 12 feet above the level of the others, so as to afford unobstructed views of the river.

As many as 600 men at a time were occasionally engaged in the works, and during the thirteen years no less than twenty lives were lost, including that of the original designer, in addition to three deaths from what is known as 'caisson disease,' that is, disease induced by working in greatly compressed air. One fearful accident occurred. 'On June 19, 1878, one of the great strands broke loose from its New York anchorage, carrying with it the "shoe" and its ponderous attachments. As the, end swept from its anchorage, it dashed off several of the men at work, and then, with a frightful leap, grazing the houses and peopled streets below, it landed for the instant in the bridge yard close under the New York tower. The great weight mid-stream whizzed it over the tower with frightful and increasing rapidity, and the whole span plunged madly into the river, narrowly missing the ferry-boats that ply, crowded with human freight, below the line of the bridge.'[1]

But it is time we crossed the bridge ourselves, and as we do so we observe that Brooklyn, though in some respects a suburb of its older neighbour, occupies a much larger site, and has ample room for that rapid expansion which is taking place. It already covers an area of more than twenty square miles, and the population, which in 1800 numbered only 2,378, had increased in 1890 to 804,377. The chief business street is Fulton Street, extending from Fulton Ferry through East New York, a distance of over seven miles. The finest residences are in the neighbourhood of Clinton Avenue and Montague Terrace, from whence very fine views of the harbour and New York are obtained. In Brooklyn, however, the various districts are not quite so sharply defined as in New York. But many more traces still remain of the old life, in the way of wooden houses, and considerable stretches of land comparatively unoccupied. But Brooklyn is sharing in the architectural revival and development which has done and is doing so much for New York; and in many parts fine business premises, handsome churches, and substantial residences are springing up.

The City Hall, County Court House, and other public buildings, stand at the junction of Fulton and Court Streets. Among the many churches for which the city is famed special mention must be made of Plymouth Church, of which Henry Ward Beecher was pastor, the Church of the Pilgrims, and the Clinton Avenue, all Congregational, and the Church of

---

[1] 'The Brooklyn Bridge,' by William C. Conant, in *Harper's Magazine* for May, 1883. This paper is full of interesting details connected with the structure of the bridge.

VIEW OF THE BRIDGE FROM THE NEW YORK SIDE.

the Holy Trinity, Episcopal.   The Young Men's Christian Association has a very fine building at the corner of Fulton Avenue and Bond Street.

Two very noted resorts are Prospect Park and Greenwood Cemetery. The former, containing 516 acres, lies in a situation of great natural

GREENWOOD CEMETERY.

beauty along a ridge, and commands a succession of very lovely views. Wood abounds, and art has done a great deal to heighten the natural charms of the place.   There are eight miles of drives, four miles of bridle-paths, and eleven miles of walks.   Here, in the spring and early summer, may be seen equipages of many kinds, the fast trotter attached to the light buggy being often very much in evidence. The Park occupies part of the site of one of the battles fought during the struggle for Independence.

Greenwood Cemetery has a world-wide fame, due partly to the great natural beauty of its situation, and partly to the many noted interments which have here taken place and the number of handsome monuments it contains. It possesses scenery of a higher order even than Prospect Park, and all that trained skill in landscape gardening and watchful care can accomplish is constantly done to preserve and to heighten the effect of the natural beauties. Since the opening in 1843 more than 250,000 interments have taken place, and it would be hard to find in any land lovelier or more peaceful resting-places than those afforded by the diversified hills and valleys and plains embraced within its limits. The area included is 474 acres, and there are no less than nineteen miles of carriage roads and seventeen miles of footpaths.

From Harper's Magazine.   Copyright, by Harper & Brothers.

APPROACH TO NEW YORK BY THE HUDSON.

THE PURITAN.

CHAPTER II.

NEW ENGLAND.

BUNKER HILL MONUMENT.

THE traveller who wishes, after making himself familiar with New York and Brooklyn, to explore the vast country comprised within the limits of the United States, has an almost bewildering choice of routes, before him. He can go West, and visit such modern marvels as Chicago and Denver, the grand gorges of the Rocky Mountains, and the natural wonders of the Yellowstone Park. He can go to the sunny and semi-tropical South, visiting on the way Washington, the seat of the Federal government, Richmond, the city around which raged so many sanguinary conflicts during the civil war, and New Orleans, where the currents of French, negro and Anglo-Saxon life have so intermingled as to produce very strange and yet withal fascinating types of character and civilisation. But if his wish be to gain a fair and accurate knowledge of the power and capabilities of the American people, he will be wise to make his first journey a visit to New England. There lived and died the

The Elms, Yale University.

men who have stamped their personality ineffaceably upon the national character. There he will come in contact with some of the strongest and most highly developed educational and literary forces; and there he will see the results of two centuries and a half of a life which, beginning with the advent of the Pilgrim Fathers, has branched out into the strong,

A STAIRCASE ON THE STEAMER PURITAN.

vigorous republican life of to-day. In the South he will meet with much which is abnormal, and in the West with much which, though full of life and vigour, is raw and crude and rudimentary. It is, therefore, desirable, if he would form any accurate judgment upon the country as a whole, to be able to fall back upon his impressions of the antiquity and culture, the education and social development, of Boston and Salem and Cambridge and Yale.

Boston, which if not, as its admirers assert, 'the hub of the universe,' is certainly the centre and capital not only of Massachusetts, but of the whole group of New England States, is within very easy reach of New York. A few hours comfortably passed in a Pullman or in an ordinary car, whilst the train runs through very pleasant and varied scenery, are sufficient for the journey of 234 miles. The pleasantest, and for Europeans the most novel route, especially in summer, is by the 'Fall River Line.' The greater part of the journey in this case is by water, and the stranger is enabled to study at his leisure, and to test the varied comforts and conveniences of one of the far-famed river steamboats. The great rivers and inland waterways of the United States have led to such a development of this branch of shipbuilding, that in no other part of the world are such enormous and luxurious steamers to be seen. The route is up the East River, and then between the picturesque shores of Long Island Sound to Fall River, and thence by train to Boston. To save time the journey is, unfortunately, made by night. The finest vessel on this line at the present date (1891), and probably the finest river steamboat in the world, is the Puritan. She is 420 feet long, 52 feet wide, and from the keel to the dome which encloses the enormous working-beam, 70 feet high, drawing when loaded 13 feet of water. There are four decks, and very spacious saloons. Intended primarily for night traffic, special attention has been paid to sleeping accommodation, and there are 355 state rooms, many of them fitted up exactly like a handsome room in an hotel or private house. Altogether no less than 1200 passengers can sleep on board. The interior decoration of this floating palace is finely designed, and has been completed in materials of the finest quality. The vessel is propelled by paddle-wheels, which are enclosed in the upper structure, and are driven by engines of 7500 horse-power. Leaving the pier on the Hudson at 5 P.M., a pleasant hour or two may be spent in watching the Sound studded with shipping, and the ever-changing shores. A very good dinner may be had in the large and handsome dining saloon. When ready to sleep, you enter a comfortable state-room, and on awaking a few hours later you find yourself at Fall River, in the limits of the State which possesses Plymouth Rock.

This place holds a position in the history of the United States and of the world secure for all time, since it represents the real birthplace of the nation. No enterprise could well have seemed more forlorn, or more certainly doomed to failure, than the landing of that little band of weary men and women who hailed even the bleak coast, of what was ever afterwards to be known as New England, as a welcome relief from the discomforts and perils of the stormy Atlantic. Already English colonists had laid a firm grasp upon the American continent in Virginia; and even in the Cape Cod district there had been previous attempts at settlement.

These men had not come to seek for gold mines, nor in the expectation of rapidly making their fortunes. They were actuated by no worldly motives, they were influenced by none of the common ambitions. Devout, godly, trained in the good school of persecutions manfully endured for righteous- ness' sake, with John Robinson's noble words of parting enshrined for ever in their hearts, they were fit instruments in God's hands for laying broad and well the foundations of a new commonwealth in which all men should have equal rights, and in which in all matters of religion the individual conscience, educated by the Word of God and illumined by the Holy Spirit, should be the supreme guide. The millions who are now so rapidly pos- sessing the splendid natural inheritance of the United States can never be

THE BURYING HILL, PLYMOUTH.

too grateful for God's providential ordering that the dominant tone and bent of the American people should come from New England rather than Virginia.

Plymouth to-day is a little town of 7000 to 8000 inhabitants, picturesque in situation, but of importance solely from the occurrence there of that potent seventeenth century event. All great enterprises rich in blessing to posterity involve sacrifice. Less than half of the original one hundred and two settlers survived the first winter. But they were not unwilling that it should be so, in order, to use the phrase of one of them, that they 'might be stepping-stones to others.' They were following the highest law, and in the whole course of their history the guiding hand of Divine Providence may be clearly traced. Driven from Scrooby in Nottinghamshire to Leyden; trained there under John Robinson, one of the noblest pastors whose

E

ministry ever enriched human hearts; disciplined by persecution, by poverty, by suffering for righteousness' sake, these Pilgrim Fathers were made of very different stuff from the dissolute adventurers, godless sailors and hungry speculators who formed so large an element in the Virginia colonies. It was on September 6, 1620, that the Mayflower finally sailed from Plymouth. One birth and one death during the hard two months' voyage kept the company at its original number. On November 9 they sighted Cape Cod, and at first tried to carry out their original intention of making the mouth of the Hudson. But falling the next day among the dangerous shoals of that unfriendly coast, they turned, sailed round the extremity of the cape, and on November 11 cast anchor in Cape Cod Harbour at the place now called the Harbour of Provincetown. Troubles on matters of discipline which had arisen thus early, led to the drawing up and signing by all the men, except seven servants who were the cause of the trouble, of an agreement, in which they assert 'we haveing undertaken for ye glorie of God, advancement of ye Christian Faith, and honour of our king and countrie, a voyage to plant ye first Colonie in ye Northern part of Virginia, doe by these presents solemly and mutualy in ye presence of God, and one of another, covenant and combine ourselves together into a civill body politick for our better ordering, and preservation, and furtherance of ye ends aforesaid: and by virtue hereof to enacte, constitute, and frame such just and equall lawes, ordinances, acts, constitutions and offices, from time to time, as shall be thought most meete and convenient for ye generall good of ye Colonie, unto which we promise all due submission and obedience.' The first landing was made upon the extremity of Cape Cod, the men going ashore for the purpose of exploration, the women to wash the clothes after the discomforts of the long voyage. More than a month was spent in prospecting before the final choice of a site for the new settlement was made. On December 6 (Old Style) the last search party started in a shallop, and after narrowly escaping shipwreck landed on Clark's Island, spent Sunday the tenth there, and on December 11 Old Style, December 21 New Style, entered Plymouth Harbour, and selected that place as the site of their new home.

Owing to a miscalculation in 1769, when the Landing of the Pilgrim Fathers was first commemorated, or, according to others, owing to a mistake in punctuation in Mourt's *Relation*, one of the contemporary narratives, the event until quite recently was celebrated on December *22nd*, one day later than the true time. On Monday, December 25, Old Style, January 4, 1621, New Style, Mourt's *Relation* tells us 'we went on shore, some to fell timber, some to saw, some to rive, and some to carry: so no man rested all that day.' It is with the landing of this party that Plymouth Rock has to do. Tradition, which in this case appears to be well supported, divides the honour of being the first to jump upon the rough landing-place between

THE RETURN OF THE MAYFLOWER TO ENGLAND.

John Alden and Mary Chilton. It was not until March 21 that the last of the colonists left the ship. And these last, no less than the first, had need of courage and dependence upon God. Exposure, want of proper food and shelter, and consequent illness, carried off six in December, eight in January, seventeen in February, and thirteen in March—forty-four, or nearly half the number, in four months. Well might Robinson in Leyden write, when the sad tidings reached him, 'In a battle it is not looked for but that divers should die. It is thought well for a side if it get the victory, though

PLYMOUTH ROCK.

with the loss of divers, if not too many or too great. God, I hope, hath given you the victory after many difficulties.' God did give the victory, but only a few of that forlorn hope lived to see it.

Plymouth Rock has not been allowed to lie undisturbed. In 1775 an attempt to remove it to the town square ended in the rock being broken into two pieces. In 1834 one piece was placed before Pilgrim Hall; the other, still in its original site, was covered over with a handsome granite canopy, into the upper story of which were gathered some of the bones of the original settlers. In Pilgrim Hall is a collection of interesting relics connected with the humble daily life of the men who laid so well and so broad the foundations of New England, and thus did so much for the United States and for the world.

The centre of life and influence in Massachusetts did not long remain at Plymouth. Boston was settled in 1630, by a company who came from Charlestown under the leadership of John Winthrop, a famous name in early colonial annals. In 1635 a Mr. Blackstone, who seems to have been the first white inhabitant of the peninsula upon which Boston stands, sold his claim for about thirty pounds. The first wharf was built in 1673; on April 24, 1704, the first newspaper, the *Boston News Letter*, appeared; and on the outbreak of trouble between the Colonies and the mother country,

THE STATE HOUSE, BOSTON.

Boston became one of the great centres of hostility to English policy. The original settlement was made upon the peninsula, called by the Indians *Shawmut*, meaning 'Sweet Waters,' but named by the Colonists Trimountain or Tremont. The area, about 700 acres, was occupied by three hills, Beacon, Copp's and the Fort. In recent times the city has overflowed into the surrounding country and now embraces Boston proper, East Boston, South Boston, Roxbury, Charlestown, Brighton, and West Roxbury; in all about 22,000 acres. The harbour, which includes about 75 square miles, abounds in islets, and is very picturesque.

In the old portion of the city the streets, as usual, are somewhat irregular and often narrow. The great fire of 1872 was not an unmixed evil, since it raged fiercely over this quarter and swept away many structures, afterwards replaced by better. The centre, and one of the most attractive

THE OLD STATE HOUSE, BOSTON.

parts of Boston, is the Common, a park forty-eight acres in extent, well laid out. This open space has in recent years been largely augmented by the addition of the public garden containing twenty-two acres. To the east of this great city lung lie the old historic portions of the city; to the west the newer and more fashionable quarter containing Commonwealth Avenue and the neighbouring streets, where are to be found the mansions of the wealthy inhabitants, and the newest and largest hotels.

Overlooking the north side of the Common, on Beacon Hill, stands the State House. The entrance hall is enriched with statues of such Massachusetts patriots as Samuel Adams, Andrews, the great 'war governor,' and Charles Sumner. There also is to be seen a large collection of the battle flags borne to victory upon many a hard-fought field in the Civil War by the eager and capable Massachusetts soldiers. Here the Legislature meets, and all the State, as distinct from Federal, business is transacted. In front of the State House, and separating it from the Common, runs Beacon Street. A more picturesque and attractive building is the old State House, situated in State Street, built in 1748 in the good old Colony times, carrying one back to the days when George III. was King, and when the great republic was unthought of. In and around this comparatively ancient building occurred many stormy scenes of the Revolutionary epoch. It is now divided between the old life and the new; the lower portions of the building are devoted to business, the upper employed as a historical museum. Other buildings connected very closely with the early life of Boston are Faneuil Hall, 'the cradle of liberty,' the only serious rival to Independence Hall, Philadelphia. It was built in 1742, and presented to the town by a Huguenot merchant, whose name it commemorates. Burnt in 1761, it was rebuilt in 1768, and enlarged in 1805.

FANEUIL HALL.

In Washington Street stands another relic of Colonial days, the old South Church. This was built in 1729, and because of its size was frequently used for public meetings in the exciting days preceding 1776. While Boston was held by the British troops the building was used as a place for cavalry drill. It ceased long ago to be used as a church. The representative of the old building in the churches of to-day is the handsome structure which adorns Boylston Street, and is known as the new Old South Church. In the older part of Boston are found many handsome piles of building, such as the City Hall, Post-office, Quincy Market, Horticultural Hall, which testify alike to the wealth, corporate life and active business of the city.

The handsomest quarter of Boston from the modern point of view is the district of which Commonwealth Avenue is the centre. Here the streets are very wide, bordered with trees, and all laid out in the latest and most approved rectangular style. The houses are all well built, well kept, and evidently within the reach only of those whose purses are heavy. In this quarter is the Public Library, exceeded in size only by the Congressional Library in Washington, the Museum of Fine Arts, the home of the Society of Natural History, and many other edifices which testify to the educational advantages and intellectual development of the Bostonians. The most imposing buildings in this region are ecclesiastical, and chief among these is the modern representative of the Old South Church already referred to, and Trinity Church, the pulpit of which has been so long and so brilliantly occupied by the Rev. Phillips Brooks. This magnificent structure was completed in 1877 at a cost of £150,000. It is one of the largest, handsomest, and most splendidly decorated churches in the United States.

OLD SOUTH CHURCH, BOSTON.

Boston has filled much space in the historic past of the United States; in all matters connected with education she has ever been in the forefront; and in all probability it must be very long before her literary pre-eminence can be very seriously challenged. It was a true instinct that led Winthrop and his followers to fix their home at Boston only ten years after the settlement of Plymouth. Here, and not on the bleak coast line, was to be one of the great centres of national life. During the early part of the eighteenth century friction between the Colonists and the Government in England steadily increased. The leaders and statesmen in England, with a few conspicuous exceptions, failed entirely to understand either the enormous vitality of the new Colonial life, or the independent way in which they were

NEW OLD SOUTH AND TRINITY CHURCHES, BOSTON.

beginning to judge political ideas and the old country's claims. In 1747 an ill-judged attempt on the part of an English commodore to put the press-gang methods into force on the Boston streets led to a disturbance, which not only compelled the return of the pressed men, but also greatly developed Colonial views on such questions as the right of personal liberty, and the rights and powers of the King of England's officers in New England. When the statesmen of George III.'s Cabinet chose to disregard all warnings, and to ride roughshod over the very delicate ground of taxation, Boston became the centre of resistance. The bitter feelings on both sides were intensified when in 1768 four regiments of British soldiers were quartered in Boston in the vain hope of overawing the town into submission. Conflicts between the townsmen and the soldiers were frequent, and in 1770 these culminated in a struggle, to be known in history as the 'Boston Massacre,' in which the soldiers fired upon the citizens, killing five persons and wounding six others.

Side by side with irritating causes of this kind, the great constitutional struggle regarding taxation had been proceeding. The colonists held the sound maxim that so long as they were unrepresented in the House of Commons, that body had no right to tax them, and that all taxes should be levied through the proper Colonial agencies. This contention the English king and his ministers obstinately disregarded. In 1765 the notorious Stamp Act was passed. By this enactment every business document in the colonies was declared illegal and void, unless it were written upon paper which bore a government stamp. The lowest value stamp was one shilling, and the more important the document the higher the stamp. So strenuous and so general was the resistance to this Act, that in 1766 it was repealed. But all the mischief it could possibly do, without benefiting the English Treasury to the extent of a single farthing, was most successfully accomplished. The colonists had already entered into the self-denying ordinance that so long as they were compelled to pay duties upon the import of articles from England, they would decline to import at all. This shut out tea and many other articles. Meanwhile attempts were made in England to repeal the tea duties, but without success.

On November 28, 1773, the Dartmouth, carrying a cargo of tea, reached Boston. The next day a meeting was called in Faneuil Hall, and this not being big enough, adjourned at once to the old South Church, and carried, on the motion of Samuel Adams, the resolution 'that the tea should not be landed, that it should be sent back in the same bottom to the place from which it came; and that no duty should be paid upon it.' Shortly after two more tea-ships arrived. The town Committee would not allow the tea to be landed, the governor would not give the pass necessary for the return of the vessels to England, the English admiral closed the Channel with his fleet, so that no vessel unprovided with a pass could leave the harbour. On the night of December 18, the ships were boarded by parties of resolute men who took possession of them, and who rapidly emptied the contents of every tea-chest in the three ships into the water of Boston Harbour. In this summary fashion they settled, once and for all, not only the tea duty but also the important question of entire freedom from the control of Great Britain. The working out cost years of suffering and bloodshed, but the decisive blow was struck on that December night.

Lord North's reply was a virtual declaration of war. On March 14, 1774, he passed what was called the Boston Port Bill, enjoining that on and after June 18 no vessels should be loaded or unladen in Boston Harbour. General Gage, the new governor, arrived in Boston in April 1774, and from that time civil war was certain, though no man could tell how or when the first blow would be struck. Nearly a year passed before the fatal moment came. On the night of April 18, 1775, Gage sent a detachment of 800 men to seize the guns and destroy the stores accumulated by the Colonists at Concord. Early on the morning of the nineteenth the opposing forces met on Lexington Common. After a short conflict seven Colonists and one English soldier lay dead on the field. The detachment reached Concord, and accomplished its object. But the whole country was alarmed, and on the return march the English lost in the desultory warfare that was kept up along the line of march, no less than sixty-five killed, one hundred and seventy-eight wounded, and twenty-eight missing—a total of 221. The entire Colonial loss was eighty. The immediate result of this conflict was the siege of Gage in Boston, the consolidation of the Colonial army under General Washington, the Battle of Bunker Hill, and the birth of the United States.

Upon an eminence in that district of Boston known as Charlestown, stands a monument visited by all strangers who care for historical associations. It possesses no beauty of any kind. It is a plain, massive, ugly obelisk of Quincy granite, 221 feet high and 30 feet square at the base. It was dedicated in 1843, President Tyler and his cabinet being at the ceremony, and Daniel Webster delivering the oration. It commemorates the first pitched battle between the Colonial and British troops. The Lexington fight was a series of skirmishes, in which the Colonists fought behind hedges and walls, and had the British at a great disadvantage. The battle of Bunker's Hill was brought about by the Colonists' seizing what was known as Breed's Hill, and fortifying it. Gage thought it essential that they should be dislodged. This was done, but at a terrible cost. The British were twice repulsed, and a third attack was successful, mainly because the Colonial ammunition was exhausted. In the closing moments of the battle Joseph Warren, the most energetic and able of the Colonial leaders, was killed. In this conflict the English lost 224 killed, and 830 wounded, or nearly half the force engaged. The Colonists lost 150 killed, 270 wounded and 30 prisoners. It soon became evident that Boston could not be held, and on March 17, 1776, it was evacuated. The city had played a prominent part in the great world drama which was being enacted, and can never lose its high place in the story of how the scattered American Colonies came to be the great United States.

Boston has long been recognised as a chief centre of educational and literary influence in the United States. In Dorchester, according to the most probable evidence, the first school supported directly out of public funds was founded; and in the Boston of to-day, into which in 1870 Dorchester was merged, we find the public educational system of the United

States in one of its most highly developed and efficient forms. On June 22, 1889, a remarkable celebration took place in Dorchester. A great gathering commemorated the 250th anniversary of the founding of Dorchester School. Schools had previously been established on the Continent; at Charles City, Virginia, in 1621; at Manhattan, a Dutch school, in 1633; what is now the Boston Latin School, in 1635; at Salem, in 1637; and at Newbury, in 1639. All these were on the model of either private schools or the old English Grammar Schools. On May 30, 1639, the inhabitants of Dorchester met in town's meeting and voted twenty pounds a year for ever 'toward the maintenance of a school in Dorchester,' to be paid yearly to 'such a schoolmaster as shall undertake to teach English, Latin, and other tongues, and also writing. The said schoolmaster to be chosen from time to time by the freemen, and it is left to the discretion of the elders and the seven men for the time being whether maids should be taught with the boys or not.' As a matter of fact the maids were not 'taught with the boys' until 1784, but this record is the earliest extant of the system of public education which now extends over the whole republic.

To-day Boston exhibits the peculiar methods and advantages of free state-aided education in a very attractive form. She possesses one Normal College in which nearly 200 girls are trained as teachers; ten Latin and High Schools with 112 teachers and 3213 scholars; fifty-five Grammar Schools with 714 teachers and 31,777 scholars; four hundred and seventy-two Primary Schools with 472 teachers and 23,832 scholars; and twenty-four Kindergarten Schools with 46 teachers and 1362 scholars. This makes a grand total for a town of nearly 450,000 inhabitants, of 562 schools, 1352 teachers, 60,367 scholars. In addition to these there are two special schools and twenty-two evening schools, with 182 teachers and 5636 scholars. In these carefully graded schools every boy and girl in Boston is provided with a thoroughly good educational training for the work of life, without the expenditure on the part of the parents of one penny beyond the quota contributed to the town's taxes. The most recent development is the inclusion of Kindergartens in the system, and it now takes the tiny urchins of three or four years, and begins to impress good discipline and correct ways of thinking upon them, and then provides all the needful steps up to the finished training of the Latin and High Schools.

Boston has for one of her nearest neighbours the town of Cambridge, the seat of the oldest and wealthiest, and in many respects the most influential, University on the Continent. Harvard College was founded in 1636 by a vote of the General Court of the Colony of Massachusetts Bay, which appropriated £400 for the endowment of a college, and in 1637 ordered that it should be established at 'Newetowne.' A school seems to have been started in the same year. It is not certain that the £400 voted was ever paid, but the movement from the first elicited private benefactions.

In 1638 John Harvard, a graduate of Emmanuel College, Cambridge, died in Charlestown, and bequeathed his entire library and half his estate to the infant college.   The bequest amounted to about £700, a large sum in those days, and out of gratitude the college took Harvard's name and 'Newetowne' was changed into Cambridge, after the *alma mater* of John Harvard.   From that time onwards the college has grown in funds, in teaching power, in numbers, and in adaptation to the educational requirements of succeeding generations. It is now the resort of many of the wealthy young men of America, and shares both the advantages and disadvantages connected with undergraduates

SEVER HALL, HARVARD.

of that class.   At the same time it would be a great mistake to imagine that it is exclusively for this class, and that the poor and hard-working student cannot take the Harvard course with advantage.   In the language of one of the official handbooks of the University, Harvard is 'the place above all others where a poor man with health and intellectual force may live inconspicuously and well on a small income which, after he becomes known, may be mainly earned by him during the year in which it must be spent.'

Harvard University now includes the College, the Graduate, Divinity, Law, and Scientific Schools, all situated in Cambridge; and the Medical, Dental, Veterinary Medicine Schools, with the Bussey Institution, a school of agriculture and horticulture which are all situated in Boston.   The property of the University amounts to nearly £2,500,000. The teaching staff consisted in 1891 of 75 professors, 22 assistant professors, and 147 other instructors of various grades; the students numbering 2271. The Library, at the head of which is Mr. Justin Winsor, LL.D., editor of the great *Narrative and Critical History of America*, contains 376,000 bound volumes, and nearly an equal number of pamphlets. Of the 300 books bequeathed by John Harvard in 1638 only *one* has survived, and that probably owes its existence to the fact that it was in the hands of a borrower when a disastrous fire in 1764

THE LAW SCHOOL, HARVARD.

destroyed the rest. It is entitled *Christian Warfare against the Devil, World, and Flesh*, folio, 1634.

The buildings of the University present great varieties in the style of their architecture. Those that have come down from the earlier times are severely plain, and remarkable more for their usefulness than for any beauty of design or finish. But many of the later structures, such as Gore Hall and Sever Hall, are not only well equipped for their special work, but are also additions to the architecture of the country. The pile that in many ways appeals most to the stranger is the Memorial Hall, the munificent gift of Harvard's sons, dedicated to the memory of the alumni who fell in the great Civil War. It was begun in 1870 and completed in 1876, at the cost of £100,000. It is 310 feet long and 115 feet wide, and is built of brick faced with buff sandstone. A tower rises from the centre 35 feet square and 200 feet high. The Memorial Hall proper occupies the centre of the pile, and is a handsome apartment with marble floor and vaulted roof. Along the walls are twenty-eight marble tablets, enclosed in arches of black walnut, and upon these are inscribed the names of the students and graduates who gave up their lives for their country in the sanguinary struggle of the Civil War. To the east of this chamber, consecrated thus to the memory of youthful

MEMORIAL HALL, HARVARD COLLEGE.

patriotism, is the Sanders Theatre, capable of seating over 1500 persons; to the west the Dining Hall, in which nearly 700 can be accommodated.

In connection with Harvard and the other great universities, there are many features of American College life upon which one would like to dwell, such, for example, as the Phi Beta Kappa and kindred societies, the commencement ceremonies, the class groupings and fellowships, the love of rhetoric and song, but the rigid limits of space forbid.

Cambridge, now containing about 70,000 inhabitants, is one of the pleasantest towns in the Eastern States, and, as being the seat of the oldest American University, is naturally rich in historical and literary associations. Under the old elm, still standing, George Washington took command of the

Colonial forces, an event commemorated by the tablet which runs: 'Under this tree Washington first took command of the American Army, July 3rd, 1775.' Close beside the aged elm is the handsome building in which now worships the church originally founded in Cambridge in 1636, and called the Shepard Memorial Church, after the first minister. Many of the houses possess historic associations. In Elmwood, built about 1760, resided the last English Lieutenant-Governor, Thomas Oliver; during the Revolution it was used as a hospital; it is now the home of James Russell Lowell, and in it the famous *Biglow Papers* were written. But by far the richest homestead in Cambridge from this point of view is Longfellow's house. It was built in 1739, and here, in 1775, Washington established his headquarters. From that day to this it has seen entering and leaving its portals many of the world's famous men. Benjamin Franklin and Talleyrand have visited here. Jared Sparks the historian, Edward Everett the orator, and Joseph E. Worcester the lexicographer, have all resided here. In 1837 Longfellow took it, and in 1843 he purchased it and made it his homestead. Here he lived in ever-increasing honour and affection until his death in 1882.

For many years the literary life of the United States centred largely in and

The Dining Hall, Memorial Hall, Harvard.

around Boston, and many of the men and women who have risen to fame in the Republic by the use of the pen resided in or near it. The mere mention of such names as Longfellow, Hawthorne, Holmes, Whittier, Lowell, to say nothing of later writers, such as Henry James, Howells, Miss Alcott, and a host of others, is sufficient evidence of this. Yet it was certain that in a country where education is so diffused varying schools of literature would spring up, as they have during the last thirty years, under writers like Mark Twain, Bret Harte, Walt Whitman, and the many minor writers who contribute to the chief magazines, and nowadays in several respects New York has succeeded to the literary pre-eminence of Boston. It would be a pleasant study to trace the many features of interest in American life presented by the poems

F

of Longfellow and Whittier and Lowell, or to trace the speciality that gives such freshness to Bret Harte, or G. W. Cable, and others of the present generation. But we have regretfully to remember that our present purpose

LONGFELLOW.

is to deal with the surface-features of the country as presented in landscape and city and custom, rather than to explore the subtler sources of thought and feeling from whence comes that which is best in the literature of a country.

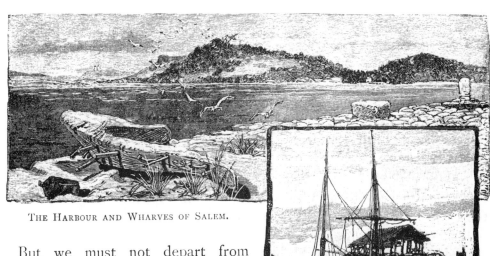

THE HARBOUR AND WHARVES OF SALEM.

But we must not depart from the neighbourhood of Boston without paying a visit to Salem, a town second in charm to none in New England, and inseparably associated not only with the earliest settlers, but also with one of the rarest literary geniuses the Western World has yet produced. A short railway ride over the bleak coast-lands lying to the north-east of Boston brings the traveller to Salem. It was settled in 1626, and in 1628 John Endicott came out from England as Governor. In June, 1629, an expedition consisting of six ships, and bringing about four hundred men, women, and children as new settlers, arrived at Salem. They had obtained a royal patent, and were styled 'The Governor and Company of the Massachusetts Bay in New England.' The aim of the company is given in the first letter of instructions sent to Endicott: 'the Propagating of the Gospel is the thing we do profess above all to be our aim in settling this Plantation.' In July, 1629, a town meeting was held 'for choyce of a pastor,' and the vote was taken 'by each one writing in a note the name of his choice.' This, Bancroft holds, was the first exercise of the ballot in America. They also all solemnly bound themselves to observe the following covenant : 'We covenant with the Lord and one with another, and do bind ourselves in the presence of God, to walk together in all His ways, according as He is pleased to reveal Himself unto us in His blessed Word of Truth.' In 1630, Winthrop, with eleven ships and 700 settlers, touched at Salem, but not liking the outlook ultimately went to Boston. Among those who accompanied Winthrop was Roger Williams, a man destined to a stormy and chequered career in the infant colony. Religious toleration in the true sense of the word was unknown in the seventeenth century, as Williams was to find. Higginson, the teacher at Salem, having died in 1631, Roger Williams was chosen to succeed him. But, in consequence of his views upon religious toleration, by the influence of the Boston settlement he was ultimately driven away from the Massachusetts Bay settlements, and was thus led, though at the cost of great suffering to himself, to found Providence, Rhode Island.

The settlement grew, and in 1637 numbered 1000 souls. The course of its early history was broken only once, and for a brief period, by the outburst of frenzy known as Salem witchcraft. It began in February, 1692, in the part now named Danvers, but then called Salem Village, in the house of the Rev. Samuel Parris. His daughter, aged nine, and his niece aged twelve, began to act 'in a strange and unusual manner,' and on being pronounced 'bewitched' by the physicians they accused Tituba, a South American slave, of having bewitched them. Tituba was beaten and compelled to confess herself guilty ; then the children accused four women, who were at once thrown into prison. The infection spread rapidly. 'So violent was the popular prejudice against every appearance of witchcraft that it was deemed meritorious to denounce all that gave the least reason for suspicion. Every child and every gossip was prepared to recognise a witch, and no one could be certain of personal safety. There is good reason to believe that in some instances the vicious and abandoned availed themselves of the opportunity to gratify their corrupt passions of envy, malice, and revenge.' Cotton Mather, instead of using his influence to check the wicked superstition, exerted all his powers to fan the flame. Life was taken from the accused on evidence that at other times would have been beneath contempt. 'From March to August, 1692, was the most distressing time Salem ever knew ; business was interrupted, the town deserted, terror was in every countenance, and distress in every heart ! Every place was the subject of some direful tale, fear haunted every street, melancholy dwelt in silence in every place after the sun retired. But as soon as the judges ceased to condemn, the people ceased to accuse. Terror at the violence and guilt of the proceedings succeeded instantly to the conviction of blind zeal, and what every man had encouraged all now professed to abhor.' Belief in Satanic agency was so strong, and such a sense of panic was developed, that in the course of a few months no less than twenty innocent persons were murdered, mainly on the testimony of brainsick children and girls, and several hundred compelled to suffer imprisonment.

Salem to-day is a pleasant, homelike little town of about 30,000 inhabitants. The foreign shipping trade which once made it a busy port has long since departed, although a good coasting trade is still carried on. But the streets are wide, the houses well built, and the town is full of historical and literary associations. The common is well situated in the centre of the town, and in Essex Street, one of the chief thoroughfares, stands Plummer Hall, containing a museum of old Colonial relics. The Essex Institute possesses a fine library. Behind Plummer Hall stands a wooden hut, which encloses and preserves the frame of the first Salem church.

The first Church as a spiritual fellowship was founded in 1629 by the covenant already referred to. But the earliest structure used by the Church was built of wood in 1634, and enlarged in 1639. In 1670 a new meeting - house was built, and the original structure was devoted to other uses, and finally removed from its old site. Tradition fixed upon a building connected with a tannery near the brow of the ill-fated Witch Hill or Gallows Hill, upon which the victims of

THE ROOM IN WHICH HAWTHORNE WAS BORN.

the cruel frenzy had suffered as the veritable first Church. The whole matter was carefully investigated by the Essex Institute, with the result that the claim of the building was found to be genuine. It was taken down carefully and removed to its present site, where it stands protected from weather and wear by the wooden house which has been built over it. The original structure was 20 feet long, 17 wide, and 12 high; it is the framework of this building which has been preserved. Nothing could well be humbler than this tiny weatherworn building, but no building on the continent is more fruitful in matter for thought. It is the only one of the first meeting-houses that has survived, and it enables the observant visitor to picture more clearly to the imagination the severe, unbending, but powerful men—Endicott and his colleagues—who subdued the wilderness because they had themselves been subdued by the power of the Word of God. The stately churches and cathedrals of England, with their ceremonials and wealth, had been forsaken, and replaced to these men by meeting-houses such as this. And they rejoiced in the change, because it brought to them liberty of conscience and freedom to worship God in the way that seemed to them right and good.

Within the church are preserved a few old relics in the way of seats and portraits, and the desk upon which Hawthorne wrote *The Scarlet Letter.* This fact links together the two sets of associations in Salem which appeal most powerfully to the mind, viz., the courage and force and strong religious belief of the men who here and elsewhere laid so firmly the foundations of New England life; and the rare insight and wonderful imaginative force of Nathaniel Hawthorne, whose life is inseparable from that of Salem. Hawthorne was born in No. 21, Union Street, July 4, 1804, and his father dying when he was only four years old, his mother returned to her old home, No. 10, Herbert Street, and there Hawthorne passed many years of his life. Hawthorne's son has sketched the town in its relation to his father's work.

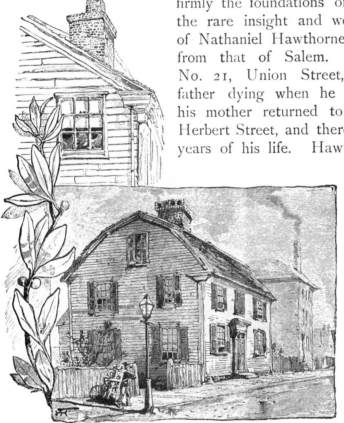

THE HOUSE IN WHICH HAWTHORNE WAS BORN.

'Numerous cross streets go from Essex Street toward two wharves; one of these is called Union Street, neat, quiet, and narrow, though with a side-walk on each side. On the western side stands the house in which Nathaniel Hawthorne was born. It is a plain clap-boarded structure of small size, with a three-cornered roof, and a single large chimney in the midst. The front is flush with the side-walk, and the high stone steps jut forth beyond. It has evidently been repaired, and now presents a very well-kept appearance; some additions have perhaps been built on in the rear, but it remains substantially unchanged; an eight-roomed house, with an attic in the gable, painted a quiet drab hue, with pale green shutters to the windows. This spot was the birthplace of a genius, but the genius itself never had an abiding-place here. It belongs to a world in which there are no places and no time, but only love and knowledge.

'Westward from Union Street lies Herbert Street; and the house in which Hawthorne lived with his widowed mother and sisters after his return from Bowdoin College stands here; the back yards of the two dwellings

NATHANIEL HAWTHORNE.

communicating. In the old time Union and Herbert Streets seem to have been practically one thoroughfare; for it was in the Herbert Street house that the words, "In this dismal chamber fame was won.—Salem, Union

Street," were written. The room in which Hawthorne wrote the *Twicetold Tales* is in the upper storey or attic.

'The genius of Hawthorne seems to have been providentially protected and trained so that it might attain its full growth and strength in an orderly

THE CUSTOM HOUSE, SALEM.

manner, without haste or eccentricity. Those lonely years in Salem were wearisome, no doubt, and often sombre; but they wrought a strength, and a self-poise in the solitary writer which all the splendour and phantasmagory of the world afterward could enrich and sweeten, but not mislead.

'From Herbert Street it is but a few steps to the Custom House, in the upper apartments of which was made the momentous discovery of Mr. Surveyor Pue's literary remains, and of the original scarlet letter, the history whereof has become more or less familiar to the educated fragment of Christendom. The building is doubtless essentially the same as it was forty years ago. Here is still the spacious edifice of brick, with the banner of the Republic, the thirteen stripes turned vertically instead of horizontally, and thus indicating that a civil and not a military sort of Uncle Sam's government is here established, floating, or drooping, in breeze or calm, from the loftiest point of its roof. Over the entrance, moreover, still hovers the enormous specimen of the American eagle, with the thunderbolts and arrows in each claw ; she is heavily gilded, and appears to be in a remarkably good state of preservation. Here too is the flight of wide granite steps descending towards the street, and the portico of half-a-dozen pillars supporting a balcony. The entrance door was closed at the time of my visit, and the neighbourhood quite

WINDOW IN SALEM CUSTOM HOUSE.

as deserted as it ever could have been in Hawthorne's day. As for the row of venerable figures, sitting in old-fashioned chairs, tipped on their hind legs back against the wall, I made no effort to discover them ; nor did I attempt to explore a certain room or office, about fifteen feet square, and of a lofty height, decorated with cobwebs and dingy paint, and its floor strewn with gray sand. The room was doubtless there, but in these days of progress and Morris wall papers its interior might have been painfully unrecognisable. In truth, I forbore to enter the Custom House at all. A more forlorn, defunct, vacant-looking place I never beheld ; and yet. it is the scene of one of the most charmingly humorous and picturesque pieces of any biographical writing in our language. The alchemy of genius never attempted to trans-

HAWTHORNE'S DESK.

mute baser metal than this into gold, or succeeded better. "The Custom House" is a fitting introduction to *The Scarlet Letter*. The original depravity of matter in the former, and of the spirit in the latter, are respectively exalted by the magic of imagination into fascination and tragic beauty.'[1]

From Salem, at the time of his marriage, Hawthorne went to reside at Concord, a little town also associated with the early history of the colonies, and also with the literary development of the nineteenth century. It was at the bridge at Concord, on April 19, 1775, that the colonial militia repulsed the expedition Gage had sent there to destroy arms and munitions, and so Concord shares with Lexington the glory of having begun

THE OLD MANSE.

the struggle during which the United States sprang into national being. It was at Concord, in the house known as ' the old Manse,' that the early years of Hawthorne's married life were passed, and the mosses that he gathered there have since enriched the substance of many minds in all parts of the civilised globe.

And now, with the whole of the vast territory of the United States yet before us, we must bid farewell to New England. One would fain visit the many points of interest along its coast, and explore the lovely scenery of the White Mountain district, and linger at Springfield, and Hartford, and the

[1] Julian Hawthorne, in *The Century*, xxviii. pp. 11-14.

WELLESLEY COLLEGE.

Valley of the Connecticut. But before we go we must hastily glance at two other great educational centres, one in Massachusetts, and one in Connecticut.

The former is Wellesley College, one of the splendid institutions for the higher education of girls, of which citizens of the United States are so justly proud. The college was established in 1875, and is situated at Wellesley, a little town upon the Boston and Albany Railroad, fifteen miles west of Boston. The college grounds embrace 300 acres of undulating and picturesque grounds, including the large and lovely expanse of water known as Lake Waban. It is 'undenominational, but distinctively and positively Christian in its influence, discipline, and instruction. The systematic study of the Bible is pursued through all the courses. Two systems of lodging are in use, the Cottage system and the Hall system. By the latter,

WABAN COTTAGE, WELLESLEY.

acquaintances are more easily made; by the former many advantages of a home are secured. The main building accommodates 330 students; Stone Hall, 108; the Cottages, 155, and a large number lodge in Wellesley; the grand total of students reaching nearly 700. The staff numbers 93, of which twelve belong to the Music School and three to the Art School; all being ladies except seven. No students under sixteen are admitted, and the classical and scientific courses extend through four years; those in Music and Art through five. As an illustration of the standard of education, we quote the requirements for the Freshman year, 1888–1889, the numbers after each subject representing the number of classes attended weekly. Latin (4) Prose Composition, Selected Letters of Cicero, Livy xxi. and xxii. (in part), Tacitus: Germania and Agricola; Greek (4), Plato: Apology and Crito, Herodotus, Selections, Odyssey, Selections; Mathematics (4), Solid and

Spherical Geometry, Advanced Algebra, Plane Trigonometry; Literature (1) Lectures on Nineteenth Century Authors; Drawing (1) from Casts; Christian Ethics (1); Bible (1) History of the Jewish Church; Elocution (1); Physiology and Hygiene, eight lectures in all.

'All students in the College buildings aid in the lighter domestic work, or in the clerical labour of the offices, libraries, and departments of instruction. Much valuable information and discipline are thus secured to the student, though the time occupied is never more than one hour daily.' The cost of board and tuition is from £70 to £80 per annum, the fees for music and art being £10 to £20 a year extra.

No surroundings could well be lovelier than those of Wellesley. Everything that the modern development of education can do to secure the physical, moral and intellectual well-being of the students is secured. The life is rather that of a college, and the students are allowed a freedom that at first seems somewhat excessive to an English mind.

BATTELL CHAPEL, YALE UNIVERSITY.

But the visitor who explores the institution under the guidance of one of the fair inmates leaves it with the strong impression that the words of the Psalmist are applicable to all its residents: 'The lines have fallen unto them in pleasant places, and they have a goodly heritage.' There are six other colleges in the Eastern States devoted to the higher education of women, the chief being Smith College at Northampton, in Massachusetts, and Vassar College at Poughkeepsie, New York. The Harvard Annex has also been established at Cambridge, to enable women to share in all the intellectual advantages of the oldest and richest University on the continent.

The other educational centre is Yale University, at New Haven, in Connecticut, the rival and in many respects the equal of Harvard. Yale College was founded in 1701 by some Connecticut ministers, and received a charter from the Colony Legislature in the same year. Under this charter a collegiate school was begun in November, 1701, at Saybrook, and removed to New Haven in 1716. It received the name of Yale in 1718, in honour of the benefactions of Elihu Yale of London. Additional charters were obtained in 1723, 1745 and 1792. In 1887, by an Act of the General Assembly of Connecticut, the title was changed from Yale College to Yale University. The courses of study embrace Philosophy and the Arts, Theology, Medicine, and Law. The Peabody Museum possesses a very fine collection of fossils. The total number of students in residence is about 1500. The grounds extend over nine acres, and are famous for their fine elms. As at Harvard, the early architecture was plain and substantial, and quite guiltless of adornment; but recently some very fine piles of building have enriched the University, the chief examples being the handsome new Battell Chapel, the Recitation Hall, the Art Building, the Peabody Museum, and Dwight Hall.

THE LAW LIBRARY IN THE CAPITOL, WASHINGTON.

TABLE AND CHAIRS USED IN CONNECTION WITH THE DECLARATION OF INDEPENDENCE.

CHAPTER III.

THE CRADLE OF INDEPENDENCE.

APART altogether from her commercial importance, and the quiet beauty
of her surroundings, the fact that Philadelphia was so closely identified
with the deliberative assemblies and acts that put an end to the Colonial
arrangements with Great Britain, gives her a unique importance among the
great cities of the Atlantic seaboard. Philadelphia is also closely connected
with the life of a great Englishman and of a great American, and with
some of the stirring movements in the old country of the seventeenth and
eighteenth centuries. William Penn, the founder of Philadelphia and of
Pennsylvania, was a son of Admiral Sir W. Penn, and was born at
Bristol in 1621. In early manhood, greatly to the chagrin of his father, he
came under Quaker influence, and was led to adopt their views; and on
behalf of these he was both able and willing to endure persecution. But,
before his death in 1670, the old admiral became reconciled to his son, and
included in the large inheritance to which Penn succeeded was a debt due
from the Crown, which in 1681 amounted to no less than £16,000. In lieu
of this sum Penn expressed his willingness to accept a grant from Charles II.
of 40,000 acres, and on March 4, 1681, a charter to this effect was drawn
up and signed. Charles, against Penn's wish, who had intended to call it

INDEPENDENCE HALL.

New Wales, named the territory covered by the charter, Pennsylvania. Penn's popularity among the Quakers, and the lofty aims he shadowed forth regarding the future government of his territory, soon attracted a large number of emigrants. On September 1, 1682, Penn set sail in the ship Welcome, carrying a hundred passengers, mostly Quakers, from Sussex. Unlike the pilgrims in the Mayflower, many died on the six weeks' voyage, thirty succumbing to small-pox. On October 27 Penn landed at Newcastle, on the Delaware. There had been for many years in this region some scattered Swedish settlements intermingled with a few Dutch colonists, but nothing in the way of a strong village or town. After a few preliminary surveys Penn sailed up the Delaware and at once selected the peninsula lying between the Delaware and the Schuylkill as the site of his capital. It was to be laid out on a large and generous scale, the houses surrounded by gardens, the streets lined with trees.

(From a portrait painted in early life.

The result has been that Philadelphia is one of the pleasantest towns to-day in the whole United States, and the one that covers the largest area. The growth was so rapid as to be phenomenal, no less than twenty-three ships full of colonists coming out in 1682.

The date of the famous treaty with the Indians, and whether it included the purchase of land, are matters upon which there has been room for differences of view. But the best authorities seem now of opinion that Penn would allow no land to be occupied until the Indian title had been acquired, and that the meeting to arrange the treaty was held at a place called Shackamaxon, June 23, 1683. Considerable territory was acquired, and the lasting friendship of the Indians won. Penn's own account is as follows : 'When the purchase was agreed, great promises passed between us of kindness and good neighbourhood, and that the Indians and English must live in love as long as the sun gave light. Which done, another made a speech to the Indians in the name of all the Sachamakers, or Kings : first, to tell them what was done ; next, to charge and command them to love the Christians, and particularly live in peace with me, and the people under my government ; that many governors had been in the river, but that no governor had come himself to live and stay here before ; and having now such an one that had treated them well, they should never do him or his any wrong —at every sentence of which they shouted and said *amen* in their own way.'

In 1684 Penn returned to England, owing to a dispute with Lord Baltimore as to the boundary between Maryland and Pennsylvania, and he was unable to return until 1699, when he came, hoping to pass the remaining years of his life in the colony. He had been absent fifteen years, but he found on his return a prosperous colony numbering 20,000 souls. But in less than two years affairs connected with the colony recalled him to London, and although he did not die until 1718 he never saw Pennsylvania again. But Philadelphia continued to prosper, and throughout the Colonial period and until the beginning of the nineteenth century it was the most important town in the country.

Hence, when, in 1774, the first Continental Congress was summoned, it was only natural that it should meet here. The members of Congress—a body, which, insignificant at first, gradually and rapidly grew in power and influence as it became more and more evident that only by united action could any sufficient check be placed upon the actions of George III. and his ministers— assembled in Philadelphia on September 5, 1774, in Carpenters' Hall, a building still standing. There were few signs at first of common feeling or action, John Adams describing the Congress as composed of 'one third Whigs, another Tories, the rest mongrel.' Nevertheless this Congress put forth a Declaration of Rights and a Petition to the King, both of which powerfully influenced the growth of public opinion. The second Congress met in Philadelphia on May 10, 1775. It was this body which appointed George Washington commander-in-chief of the colonial troops, and which organised the army to oppose the British troops at Boston and elsewhere. The third Congress, destined to become world-famous by reason of the results flowing from its legislative action, met in Philadelphia, in the State

House, a structure which we shall shortly visit, on May 12, 1776. Events had moved rapidly during the preceding eighteen months, and it was becoming increasingly clear to men's minds that independence of Great Britain was the only possible solution of present difficulties. On June 7 R. H. Lee of Virginia moved, and John Adams of Massachusetts seconded, the following resolutions :—

'That these United Colonies are, and of right ought to be, free and independent States ; that they are absolved from all allegiance to the British Crown ; and that all political connection between them and the State of Great Britain is, and ought to be, totally dissolved.

'That it is expedient forthwith to take the most effectual measures for forming foreign alliances.

'That a plan of confederation be prepared and transmitted to the respective colonies for their consideration and approbation.'

On June 10 it was resolved that consideration of the first of these resolutions be postponed till July 1, and that meanwhile a committee be appointed to draft a Declaration of Independence. The committee consisted of Thomas Jefferson, John Adams, Benjamin Franklin, Roger Sherman, and Robert R. Livingston. Jefferson's account of what happened is, that he prepared a draft which was submitted to Franklin and Adams, each of whom made a few verbal alterations. When Congress met on July 1, postponement of one day was granted at the request of South Carolina. The all-important resolution in favour of independence was carried, after a long and somewhat stormy debate, on July 2. The discussions in committee over the reasons for the declaration, extended over July 3 and 4, and it was not until late on the latter afternoon that the complete Declaration of Independence was approved, passed, and ordered to be printed. It was not until July 8 that any public celebration of this momentous event—the creation of a new Power of the first rank among the nations of the earth —took place. But on that day, amid general rejoicings, the Declaration was read to an assembly in the yard of the State House.

It is a curious fact that the two chief annual celebrations in the United States fall upon other than the true dates of the events they commemorate. We have already noted the discrepancy in the date of the Landing of the Pilgrim Fathers.[1] John Adams, in a letter to his wife which has become famous, says : 'The second day of July, 1776, will be the most memorable epoch in the history of America. I am apt to believe that it will be celebrated by succeeding generations as the great anniversary festival. It ought to be commemorated as the day of deliverance by solemn acts of devotion to God Almighty. It ought to be solemnised with pomp and parade, with shows, games, sports, guns, bells, bonfires, and illuminations, from one end of this continent to the other, from this time forward for evermore.' This

[1] See p. 50.

forecast of the man who played so prominent a part in the great event has been justified, but he could not have foreseen that the date selected would be, not that on which the great event took place, but that upon which the reasons for it were adopted. The youth of the United States joyously continue to celebrate Independence Day. The stranger who happens to pass a Fourth of July in the United States may be forgiven for wishing that it had taken some other form than the ceaseless discharge of firearms and Chinese crackers; but he would be captious indeed who would deny to

THE FIRST DRAFT OF THE DECLARATION OF INDEPENDENCE IN JEFFERSON'S HANDWRITING, AND WITH HIS OWN CORRECTIONS.

(*From the original, preserved in Washington.*)

a great people the right to celebrate the national birthday in a way which to themselves appears most suitable.

The men who ultimately signed the Declaration of Independence, fifty-six in all, were for the most part men of great influence in their respective colonies, and in many cases men well known on both sides of the Atlantic. The oldest of the band, a man then in his seventy-first year, was one of the foremost scientific discoverers of the eighteenth century, a man whose face was well known in Edinburgh, and London, and Paris; a man who had passed most of his life in Philadelphia, and to whom much of the progress of the city and also of the united colonies was due—Benjamin

In C O N G R E S S, *July* 4, 1776.

A DECLARATION

By *the* R E P R E S E N T A T I V E S *of the*

UNITED STATES OF AMERICA,

In *GENERAL CONGRESS* ASSEMBLED.

WHEN in the Courfe of human Events, it becomes neceffary for one People to diffolve the Political Bands which have connected them with another, and to affume among the Powers of the Earth, the feperate and equal Station to which the Laws of Nature and of Nature's God entitle them, a decent Refpect to the Opinions of Mankind requires that they fhould declare the Caufes which impel them to the feperation.

We hold thefe Truths to be felf-evident, that all Men are created equal, that they are endowed by their Creator with certain unalienable Rights, that among thefe are Life, Liberty, and the Purfuit of Happinefs.—That to fecure thefe Rights, Governments are inftituted among Men, deriving their juft Powers from the Confent of the Governed, that whenever any Form of Government becomes deftructive of thefe Ends, it is the Right of the People to alter or to abolifh it, and to inftitute new Government, laying its foundation on fuch Principles, and organizing its Powers in fuch Form, as to them fhall feem moft likely to effect their Safety and Happinefs. Prudence, indeed, will dictate that Governments long eftablifhed fhould not be changed for light and tranfient Caufes; and accordingly all Experience hath fhewn, that Mankind are more difpofed to fuffer, while Evils are fufferable, than to right themfelves by abolifhing the Forms to which they are accuftomed. But when a long Train of Abufes and Ufurpations, purfuing invariably the fame Object, evinces a Defign to reduce them under abfolute Defpotifm, it is their Right, it is their Duty, to throw off fuch Government, and to provide new Guards for their future Security. Such has been the patient Sufferance of thefe Colonies; and fuch is now the Neceffity which conftrains them to alter their former Syftems of Government. The Hiftory of the prefent King of Great-Britain is a Hiftory of repeated Injuries and Ufurpations, all having in direct Object the Eftablifhment of an abfolute Tyranny over thefe States. To prove this, let Facts be fubmitted to a candid World.

He has refufed his Affent to Laws, the moft wholefome and neceffary for the public Good.

He has forbidden his Governors to pafs Laws of immediate and preffing Importance, unlefs fufpended in their Operation till his Affent fhould be obtained; and when fo fufpended, he has utterly neglected to attend to them.

He has refufed to pafs other Laws for the Accommodation of large Diftricts of People, unlefs thofe People would relinquifh the Right of Reprefentation in the Legiflature, a Right ineftimable to them, and formidable to Tyrants only.

He has called together Legiflative Bodies at Places unufual, uncomfortable, and diftant from the Depofitory of their public Records, for the fole Purpofe of fatiguing them into Compliance with his Meafures.

He has diffolved Reprefentative Houfes repeatedly, for oppofing with manly Firmnefs his Invafions on the Rights of the People.

He has refufed for a long Time, after fuch Diffolutions, to caufe others to be elected; whereby the Legiflative Powers, incapable of Annihilation, have returned to the people at large for their exercife; the State remaining in the mean time expofed to all the Dangers of Invafion from without, and Convulfions within.

He has endeavoured to prevent the population of thefe States; for that Purpofe obftructing the Laws for Naturalization of Foreigners; refufing to pafs others to encourage their Migrations hither, and raifing the Conditions of new Appropriations of Lands.

He has obftructed the Adminiftration of Juftice, by refufing his Affent to Laws for eftablifhing Judiciary Powers.

He has made Judges dependent on his Will alone, for the Tenure of their Offices, and the Amount and Payment of their Salaries.

He has erected a multitude of new Offices, and fent hither Swarms of Officers to harrafs our People, and eat out their Subftance.

He has kept among us, in Times of Peace, Standing Armies, without the Confent of our Legiflatures.

He has affected to render the Military independent of and fuperior to the civil Power.

He has combined with others to fubject us to a Jurifdiction foreign to our Conftitution, and unacknowledged by our Laws; giving his Affent to their Acts of pretended Legiflation:

For quartering large Bodies of armed Troops among us:

For protecting them, by a mock Trial, from Punifhment for any Murders which they fhould commit on the Inhabitants of thefe States:

For cutting off our Trade with all Parts of the World:

For impofing Taxes on us without our Confent:

For depriving us, in many Cafes, of the Benefits of Trial by Jury:

For tranfporting us beyond Seas to be tried for pretended Offences:

For abolifhing the free fyftem of Englifh Laws in a neighbouring Province, eftablifhing therein an arbitrary Government, and enlarging its Boundaries, fo as to render it at once an Example and fit Inftrument for introducing the fame abfolute Rule into thefe Colonies:

For taking away our Charters, abolifhing our moft valuable Laws, and altering fundamentally the Forms of our Governments:

For fufpending our own Legiflatures, and declaring themfelves invefted with Power to legiflate for us in all Cafes whatfoever.

He has abdicated Government here, by declaring us out of his Protection and waging War againft us.

He has plundered our Seas, ravaged our Coafts, burnt our Towns, and deftroyed the Lives of our People.

He is at this Time, tranfporting large Armies of foreign Mercenaries to compleat the Works of Death, Defolation and Tyranny, already begun with Circumftances of Cruelty and Perfidy fcarcely paralleled in the moft barbarous Ages, and totally unworthy the Head of a civilized Nation.

He has conftrained our fellow Citizens taken Captive on the high Seas to bear Arms againft their Country, to become the Executioners of their Friends and Brethren, or to fall themfelves by their Hands.

He has excited Domeftic Infurrections amongft us, and has endeavoured to bring on the Inhabitants of our Frontiers, the mercilefs Indian Savages, whofe known Rule of Warfare, is an undiftinguifhed Deftruction, of all Ages, Sexes and Conditions.

In every Stage of thefe Oppreffions we have petitioned for Redrefs, in the moft humble Terms: Our repeated Petitions have been anfwered only by repeated Injury. A Prince, whofe Character is thus marked by every Act which may define a Tyrant, is unfit to be the Ruler of a free People.

Nor have we been wanting in Attention to our Britifh Brethren. We have warned them from Time to Time of Attempts by their legiflature to extend an unwarrantable Jurifdiction over us. We have reminded them of the Circumftances of our Emigration and Settlement here. We have appealed to their native Juftice and Magnanimity, and we have conjured them by the Ties of our common Kindred to difavow thefe Ufurpations, which would inevitably interrupt our Connections and Correfpondence. They too have been deaf to the Voice of Juftice and of Confanguinity. We muft, therefore, acquiefce in the Neceffity which denounces our Separation, and hold them, as we hold the reft of Mankind, Enemies in War; in Peace, Friends.

We, therefore, the Reprefentatives of the UNITED STATES OF AMERICA, in General Congress affembled, appealing to the Supreme Judge of the World for the Rectitude of our Intentions, do in the Name and by the Authority of the good People of thefe Colonies, folemnly Publifh and Declare, That thefe United Colonies are, and of Right ought to be, FREE AND INDEPENDENT STATES; that they are abfolved from all Allegiance to the Britifh Crown, and that all political Connection between them and the State of Great-Britain, is, and ought to be, totally diffolved; and that as FREE AND INDEPENDENT STATES, they have full Power to levy War, conclude Peace, contract Alliances, eftablifh Commerce, and to do all other Acts and Things which INDEPENDENT STATES may of Right do. And for the Support of this Declaration, with a firm Reliance on the Protection of Divine Providence, we mutually pledge to each other our Lives, our Fortunes, and our facred Honor.

Signed by ORDER *and in* BEHALF *of the* CONGRESS,

JOHN HANCOCK, Prefident.

ATTEST.

CHARLES THOMPSON, Secretary.

AMERICA: BOSTON, Printed by JOHN GILL, and POWARS and WILLIS, in QUEEN-STREET.

(From a handbill printed and publifhed in Boston.)

Franklin, printer, electrician, colonial agent, member of Congress, and finally Plenipotentiary to European Courts of the newly-born United States. A chapter on Philadelphia would be incomplete without some reference to this remarkable man.

He was born in Boston, Massachusetts, in 1706, his father having emigrated from England in 1685. He was the fifteenth child and the tenth and youngest son. He was taken from school at the age of ten and set to work in the tallow-chandler's shop kept by his father. But scanty as his schooling was, his home training was of a very high class, and he owed much to the sterling influence of his father. When about fifteen years old he became engaged in printing and publishing with his elder brother James, a newspaper called *The New England Courant.* A quarrel ensued, and in 1723 he ran away to Philadelphia. The story has often been told of how he walked through the streets eating a roll for his breakfast, carrying in his pockets all his worldly possessions, seen and laughed at by the girl who, little as she then thought, was afterwards to become his wife. But he managed to get on. The governor induced him to go to London to procure plant for a printing business, but failed to give him letters of credit which had been promised. Hence, on his arrival in London he had to take work in a printing office in Bartholomew Close. He returned to Philadelphia in 1726, became editor and publisher of the *Pennsylvania Gazette,* and began to prosper in business. *Poor Richard's Almanack,* in which he printed many of his wise saws and proverbial sayings, first appeared in 1733, and ultimately attained a very wide circulation. We give as matters of literary and historical interest facsimiles of the title-page of the first edition of the *Almanack,* and of a letter in Franklin's handwriting. The letter illustrates the strong feeling manifested upon both the Colonial and English sides in the early stages of the Independence struggle, and is a good specimen of Franklin's clear and direct style. In 1746 he met in Boston, Dr. Spence, a Scotchman, who performed some experiments in electricity for his amusement, thus introducing him to a study in connection with which he was to win world-wide fame. On his return to Philadelphia,

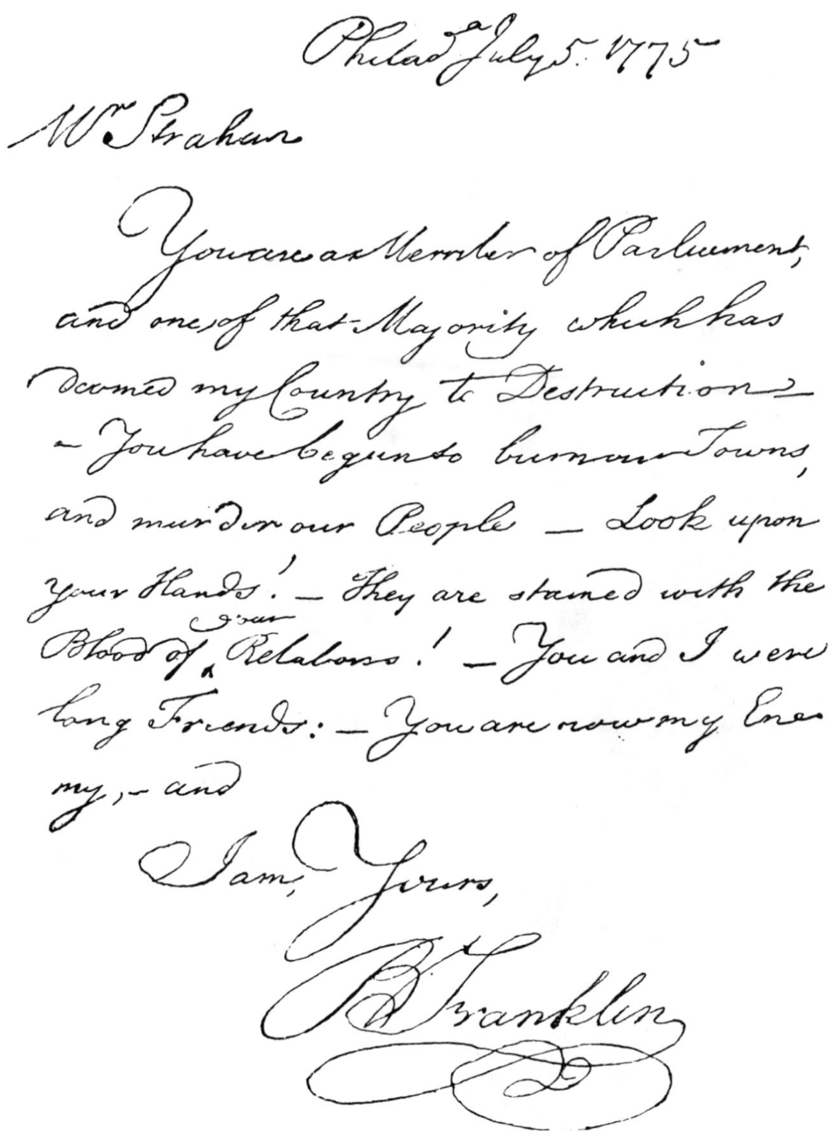

Philad July 5. 1775

Mr Strahan.

You are a Member of Parliament, and one of that Majority which has doomed my Country to Destruction — You have begun to burn our Towns, and murder our People — Look upon your Hands! — They are stained with the Blood of your Relations! — You and I were long Friends: — You are now my Enemy, — and

I am, Yours,

B Franklin

Franklin at once began investigating the matter, and arrived finally at the far-reaching conclusion that lightning and the electric spark were identical. When communicated to the Royal Society in a paper written by Franklin, this view was received with laughter; but in June 1752, on the common in Philadelphia, by the ever-memorable flying of the properly-prepared kite, in a thunderstorm he succeeded in drawing the electric spark from the cloud. This great discovery aroused immediate and wide-spread interest, and placed Franklin very high in the rank of scientific experimentalists.

During the years preceding the Revolution, he acted as London agent to the colonies, and at the Bar of the House of Commons advocated the Repeal of the Stamp Act in 1766. When, in 1775, it became evident that nothing but force would wring from the Home Government the concessions demanded by the colonists, Franklin returned to Philadelphia. He devoted much time and energy to the three great bodies of which he was a member— the Assembly of Pennsylvania, the Continental Congress, and the Committee of Public Safety. We have already referred to his share in the Declaration. In 1778 he negotiated an alliance with France, and was received in Paris officially as Ambassador of the new Power. He took a very prominent part in the negotiations carried on during 1782 for peace with Great Britain, and was one of the four who signed the Treaty of Paris in 1783 on behalf of the United States. He returned to Philadelphia in 1786, when the whole population of the city turned out to greet him. After fifty years of active and fruitful public service, he spent peacefully, and as happily as increasing infirmity would permit, the closing days of his life, passing away April 17, 1790.

BENJAMIN FRANKLIN.

As the centre of historical associations like these, Philadelphia must ever hold a foremost place among the great cities of the United States. Founded by far-seeing, shrewd and industrious Quakers, the 'City of Brotherly Love' has also attained to one of the highest places of importance in the commercial life of the Republic. It extends twenty-two miles from north to south, and five to eight miles from east to west, with a population in 1890 of 1,044,894. The great business thoroughfares run from east to west, the chief among them being Market Street. The streets crossing these run at right angles, and the whole city is laid out with almost mathematical precision. The chief thoroughfare running north and south, and occupying the central line, is Broad Street. But the thoroughfare of most interest to the visitor is Chestnut Street, a fine broad roadway lined with handsome piles of building, and containing many sites of historic importance. From the Delaware to the Schuylkill the streets are numbered in order, First, Second, Third, &c., and the line of Chestnut Street marks the direction

THE MERCHANTS' EXCHANGE, PHILADELPHIA.

of early settlement. In Second Street, for instance, a little to the north of Chestnut Street, stands the Commercial Exchange, occupying the site of the 'Slate-roof House,' one of the residences of William Penn, and in later days the home of John Adams, John Hancock, and Benedict Arnold. In the same street, a little to the south of Chestnut Street, is Christ Church, which dates from 1695; and in the graveyard on Fifth Street, belonging to this church, Franklin is buried. In this immediate neighbourhood, in Lætitia Street, stood Penn's cottage, the first brick building in Philadelphia, recently removed to Fairmount Park. In Third Street stands the handsome

Merchants' Exchange, of which we give an engraving. It is built of marble, and the façade on Dock Street shows a semicircular colonnade, within which rises a dome. Many of the chief business premises of the city are in this quarter.

Following Chestnut Street in an easterly direction we come to a narrow street nearly shut in by lofty piles of building, and at the end of the court stands a low, two storey, brick building. This is the famous Carpenters' Hall. The Carpenters' Company, modelled upon the ancient Guild of the same name in the City of London, dates from 1724, and the Hall was built in 1770, just when the colonies were beginning to face the question of political severance from Great Britian. As the State House was in possession of the governing powers, it was only natural that the new hall should be used for meetings by the colonists. Hence many town meetings were held either on the lawn in front or within the Hall. As already noted, the first Continental Congress held their sessions here. On June 18, 1776, a great convention was held here, which resulted in the Philadelphia members of Congress supporting Independence, which they had hitherto been instructed to oppose. At one time or another the voices of many of the men most prominent in revolutionary times have been heard within these walls. The Hall possesses a fine library, and is a flourishing benevolent institution, with large funds at its disposal for the relief of the widows and young children of deceased members of the guild.

Continuing our stroll, and passing the Custom House, we come to a low, two storey, red-brick building, standing back a few feet from the roadway, the centre of the space being occupied with a statue of George Washington. It is gratifying to the historic imagination to know that through the doorway, reached by a flight of four steps, George Washington himself often passed, and that, within the rooms which we are about to enter, his voice was often heard. And not his alone, but those of Patrick Henry, Samuel and John Adams, John Hancock—in short, of all the men who took any active part in the first twenty-five years of the political life of the United States. This unpretending building is Independence Hall, and this is the real 'Cradle of Independence.' It was begun in 1729, finished in 1735, and cost the modest sum of £5,600. It was in a large room on the ground floor, still preserved in much the same state as it was then, that the Congress of 1776 passed the famous Declaration, and this room has ever since been a shrine to which multitudes of devout republican pilgrims have journeyed. Upon a platform at one end of the room are preserved the table and chairs said to have been used at the signing of the Declaration. The details of this event have not been completely ascertained to the satisfaction of all, but the evidence appears conclusive that there was nothing in the way of general signing until August 2, 1776, and that then it was not the original document, but an engrossed copy of it, which was signed. From the ceiling of the fine old staircase, by which the upper rooms are reached, hangs the old 'Liberty Bell,' formerly hung in the tower which rises above the building, and said to have been rung at the moment of signing. The legend runs that it was joyously rung at the bidding of a

INDEPENDENCE HALL, FROM CHESTNUT STREET.

child. But, unfortunately, this seems to be only a legend, as also one is sorry to learn from reliable authorities are the assertions that when John Hancock signed he said, 'There, John Bull may read my name without spectacles;' and that Franklin grimly remarked, 'We must hang together, or else, most assuredly, we shall all hang separately.' In the rear of the hall is Independence Square, and from the further end of this one of the best views of the building is obtained. As we walk along Chestnut Street we pass the great hotels, Continental and Girard House, the Post Office, the United States Mint, the enormous mass of building called the Public Buildings, close by which is the large and busy station of the Pennsylvania Railway. But it is impossible for us even to name the many public institutions which enrich Philadelphia. From the earliest days private munificence has done much to benefit the citizens, and many institutions of this kind may be mentioned—the Pennsylvania Hospital, founded in 1755 by Franklin and two physicians, brothers, of the name of Bond; and the Girard College, 'for the gratuitous instruction and support of destitute orphans,' endowed by Stephen Girard, who died in 1831, leaving to it an estate now worth about £3,000,000. The grounds contain forty-two acres. Philadelphia is well supplied with educational institutions. The free school system is in force, and among the libraries may be mentioned the Ridgeway and the Mercantile, both containing very large and valuable collections.

Philadelphia is a great railroad centre, nearly all the traffic from New York to the south, and a large portion of the traffic to the west, passing through it. Perhaps the most luxurious train in the world is the Chicago Limited, on the Pennsylvania Railway, which passes through Philadelphia every day. The suburbs of Philadelphia are very pleasant, and the land for many miles to the west, to an English eye at any rate, appears much better cultivated, and presents a more settled and homelike appearance than any part of the State, except, perhaps, the neighbourhood of Boston.

Pennsylvania, especially in the westerly regions, is very rich in mineral wealth, and consequently is one of the great manufacturing centres. Harrisburg, on the Susquehanna, the capital of the State, is a handsome city of about 50,000 inhabitants, surrounded by lovely scenery. Pittsburg, still further west, is the next largest city in the State to Philadelphia, with a population of about 250,000. Lying near vast iron and coal mines, it is the Sheffield of America, and until quite recently used to be as black and as overshadowed by smoke as the English town. But the introduction of 'natural gas' has to a very great extent obviated the use of coal, to the great benefit of the atmosphere and of the lungs of the residents. The railroad from Harrisburg runs through the valley of the Juniata, affording a long succession of very lovely and picturesque views. Seventy or eighty miles to the east of Pittsburg, Johnstown is passed, the scene of the frightful disaster in May, 1889, occasioned by the bursting of a dam, which emptied a reservoir and produced a flood which swept away the greater part of the town, causing a terrible loss of life. When the writer saw the town, a year after the calamity, there were traces on every hand of the fearful character of the flood; but, with characteristic energy, much of the town had already been rebuilt.

In the north-western corner of Pennsylvania is the great petroleum-producing district of the world. It was here in 1859 that Colonel Drake first 'struck oil,' although he was in search of it for use as a patent medicine, and not as an illuminating agent. The oil-producing region is about 150 miles long, and from one to twenty miles broad; having Oil City, Titusville, and Bradford as the chief centres of population. In 1859 Colonel Drake's well yielded 2,000 barrels of oil; since that time one district has in a single year yielded as much as 22,000,000 barrels. The oil stratum lies on a level, and the depth of the well is, of course, determined by the nature of the surface, a well starting from a valley necessarily being less deep than one upon a hill. At Oil Creek oil was struck at a depth of 600 feet, at Bradford from 1,100 to 2,000, at Cherry Grove at a depth of 1,600. The oil stratum is porous sandstone, vary-

SHOOTING A WELL.

ing in thickness from five to thirty feet, thoroughly saturated with oil. As soon as a well is drilled into it, a strong pressure of natural gas forces the oil up to the surface, causing it to flow for months, and in some cases for years. The process of sinking a well is very simple. A rough timber derrick, like that shown in the engraving, is built, and attached to it is a shed for the engine and machinery, used first to work the drill and sand-pump, and then, when it becomes necessary, to pump the oil. The contract price for drilling a well is about three shillings a foot, and a well complete with all needful apparatus involves an outlay of £600 to £800. As long as the oil flows naturally all that has to be done is to preserve and store the oil. The volume of this natural yield has been known to reach the enormous amount of 4,000 barrels in twenty-four hours from a single well. When a well ceases to flow it is torpedoed, that is, a tin tube containing six or eight quarts of nitro-glycerine or dynamite is exploded at the bottom. The explosion is audible only as a pistol-shot, but the ground heaves, and very speedily the newly-liberated oil comes spurting up in a jet like that shown on page 95. All over the United States one is struck with the

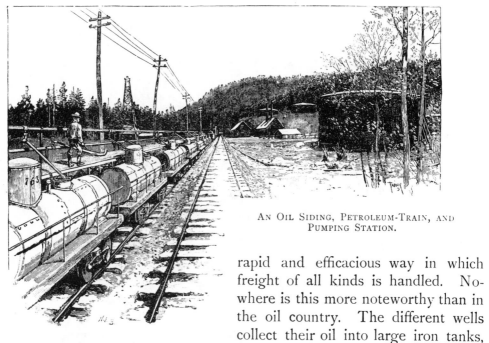

An Oil Siding, Petroleum-Train, and Pumping Station.

rapid and efficacious way in which freight of all kinds is handled. No-where is this more noteworthy than in the oil country. The different wells collect their oil into large iron tanks, and in recent years an ingenious system of pipes has been laid down, by which the contents of these storage tanks are conveyed various distances up to three hundred miles. This system is worked mainly by the United Pipe Lines Company. This company has laid down systems of pipes which extend from the oil fields straight to the refineries at such towns as Buffalo, Cleveland and Pittsburg, or to shipping centres, such as Bayonne on New York Bay, three hundred miles away from the wells. The method of working is simple and easy. When a well-tank is nearly full, one of the company's men comes, gauges the oil in the tank, opens the locked stopcock of the connecting pipe, and lets as much oil flow out as the well-owners wish to sell. Three certificates stating the quantity of oil run off are made out; one for the well manager, one goes to the central office, one is retained by the company's agent. At the central office credit is given to the well for the amount of oil run off, less three per cent. deducted for sediment and evaporation. The oil is now in possession of the company, and is mixed in their huge storage tanks with that coming from all the other wells, all crude petroleum being classed as of uniform value. When the owner wishes to use or sell the oil, it is delivered at one of the main shipping centres, and he has to pay a pipeage charge of tenpence a barrel, and a storage charge of two shillings a day per 1000 barrels.

A familiar object on the railroads in the United States is the petroleum train, of which we give an illustration. Large quantities of oil are conveyed to convenient centres by short pipe lines, and thence conveyed to the refineries by rail. The cylindrical tanks contain about 25,000 gallons each, and the cupola on top is to give space for the oil to expand when heated by the sun.

Pennsylvania, in addition to its coal and iron, is also rich in the substance known as 'natural gas.' This gas, produced in enormous quantities by the action of natural force, is stored in vast reservoirs, which are tapped in much the same way as the oil. By means of pipes this gas can be conveyed long distances, and is now used in Pittsburg and many other towns for fuel, and also for lighting purposes. It is of the greatest value as fuel, possessing none of the disadvantages of coal and wood, but its illuminating power is low, and places lit by it do not present a very attractive appearance at night.

A GAS WELL.

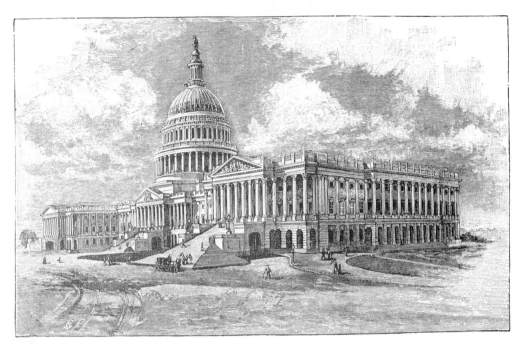

THE CAPITOL AT WASHINGTON—EAST FRONT.

CHAPTER IV.

THE FEDERAL CAPITAL.

A LOBBYIST.

AS soon as the American Colonies won their independence, the question of a national capital came to the
front, at once developing mutual jealousies, and that view
of political life which has resulted in the selection of small
towns as the site of State capitals, and which placed the
Federal Capital in what fifty years ago was described as 'a
backwoods settlement in the wilderness.' Under the influence of this feeling, Albany and not New York, Harrisburg and not Philadelphia, Springfield and not Chicago are
the capitals of their respective States, and under the influence of the same feeling a Federal Capital was built upon
the swampy morasses of the Potomac. The site of the city
was chosen in 1790. Maryland and Virginia ceded a district ten miles
square, lying upon both banks of the Potomac about one hundred miles
from its mouth. Ultimately only the Maryland portion, on the northern
bank of the river, was taken. This territory, called the District of Columbia,
contains about seventy square miles, and the site of Washington, a low-lying
bottom land for the most part, is about five miles in length and three in
breadth, and is surrounded by rolling upland country. Hither in 1800 came
the seat of Government, and from that day Washington has continued to

The Smithsonian Institution at Washington.

grow slowly but steadily in population and in favour as a place of residence for people of wealth and education and leisure.

It is reached by an easy and pleasant journey from Philadelphia, the only city of considerable importance passed on the way being Baltimore, which is delightfully situated on the Patapsco River near its entrance into Chesapeake Bay. The public institution, among the many which enrich Baltimore, most likely to interest the passing European is the University founded by the munificence of Johns Hopkins, a wealthy citizen, and called by his name. For this purpose he left land and stocks valued at about £750,000. Although opened to students only so recently as 1876, the University has already achieved high distinction. It exists mainly for higher education, aiming to begin where the ordinary university course ends,

PENNSYLVANIA AVENUE, WASHINGTON.

thus enrolling as students for the most part only 'those who have already taken an academic degree, or who have otherwise fitted themselves to pursue advanced courses of study.' The University has already achieved good work, and gives promise of much more in the future. Special publications are issued by the faculty—notably the series of *Studies in Historical and Political Science*, edited by Dr. Adams—and facilities are afforded for work of special research. In connection with the University a Johns Hopkins Hospital was opened in 1889. It consists of a group of seventeen admirably planned and equipped buildings in one of the best sites in Baltimore. In time a Medical School will be established there, when some wealthy man responds to the President's appeal for £100,000 for this purpose: appeals of this kind rarely failing to meet with ready response in the United States. Baltimore was notorious in 1861 for the riot and the attack upon the United States troops then passing through to the defence of Washington.

The railway journey from Baltimore to Washington takes only a little over an hour, and a fine view of the capital is obtained from the approaching train. Washington, whatever may have been its early state, and however slow its development, is now without question one of the handsomest cities in the United States. It was laid out on a magnificent plan, a plan which remained for over fifty years only an ideal; but in the last twenty-five years much has been done in the way of realization. The centre of the city is the Capitol, a large and imposing building standing upon an eminence, and forming the most conspicuous object in the city. From it radiate three great streets running north, east and south, known respectively as North, East and South Capitol Streets. Most

MASSACHUSETTS AVENUE, WASHINGTON.

of the streets run due north and south, or east and west, the former numbered, the latter called by the letters of the alphabet. Besides these a system of avenues, named after the States of the Union, run diagonally through the city. The thoroughfares in Washington are the widest in any large city of the world. The avenues are from 120 to 160, the streets from 80 to 120 feet wide. Possessing so much space, the great majority of the side-walks are bordered with double rows of trees, and wide sections are covered with turf. Most of the roadways, which are well made and well kept, are asphalted. The intersections of these wide thoroughfares, and the large number of additional open spaces made by the diagonal arrangement of the avenues, has given Washington a multitude of circles and squares and miniature parks, and the width of the streets gives views of great beauty at almost every turn. There are about 250 miles of streets, and the public ways occupy more than half of the entire area of the capital. In the residential sections the houses are handsome and well-built, often exhibiting very considerable architectural skill and boldness of design, and many of them stand in spacious grounds embowered in trees. The best time to see Washington is in May or June, when the trees are out in their early summer beauty.

The central thoroughfare is that part of Pennsylvania Avenue which lies between the Capitol and the Treasury, and here are found many of the chief hotels and business premises. The city has had a somewhat chequered career as regards its internal government. Originally both Georgetown, now an ntegral part of the city, and Washington had charters; but under this régime the buildings were neglected, the streets uncared for, and even as recently as 1871 the city was in a disgraceful condition. In that year Congress abolished the old charters, and appointed a governor and a legislative assembly to act with him. The governor was Alexander Shepherd, a native of Washington, and a man of great energy and ability. But his ideas far out-ran the needs of that day, and in three years he saddled the city with an enormous debt, though at the same time conferring great boons upon the citizens. Under him a board of public works was instituted, and to their efforts much of the present comfort and magnificence of Washington is due. In 1874, however, Congress again changed the form of government, and appointed three commissioners, who found that Shepherd's work had been so thoroughly begun that there was no option but to carry out his plans. This was done, resulting in a debt of £4,500,000 upon a city where the total property was worth only £20,000,000. In 1878 Congress passed a bill for the permanent government, providing that three commissioners should be appointed by the President of the United States, exercise all executive functions, and be responsible only to Congress. Hence Washington presents the strange phenomenon of a city in which the inhabitants have no voice whatever in the management of civic affairs; but at the same time it must be remembered that the city exists solely because the seat of government is there. Had it been left to the normal influences which determine the growth of cities, Washington would probably have been nothing more than a village to-day.

A stroll through the streets of Washington soon conveys the impression that it stands on the edge of the South. Washington, which in 1860 had only 60,000, has now a population of a little over 200,000, and out of that number about 65,000 are negroes. They are met with everywhere, and are sufficiently numerous to be a very distinctive feature in Washington street life. They poured into the city in great numbers during the Civil War, and, according to general testimony, form one of the most steady, sober, and industrious negro populations of the whole United States. Further south the results of negro labour are not so satisfactory; but here they have learned various trades, and are occupied in many different ways as messengers, petty clerks, household servants, hucksters, etc. They are thrifty, and put by part of their earnings; their children are educated in special schools provided for them by the State; they have their own churches, and so long as they are willing to work—and almost all of them are— plenty of occupation is within their reach. Looking upon them now it is not easy to realise that only one generation has passed since they were bought and sold like cattle under the very shadow of the Capitol.

Washington is full of vast and conspicuous public buildings, and among them the White House, the official home of the President of the United

OUTSIDE THE MARKET, WASHINGTON.

States, takes first rank. It stands in a beautiful situation. In front of the main entrance is Lafayette Square, the pleasantest of the many pleasant little parks which abound in the city. In the rear the grounds, seventy-five acres in extent, stretch away to the Potomac, and from all the windows overlooking them lovely views are enjoyed. The building, unlike most of its confrères, is not at all pretentious. It was originally intended as a suitable home for the first citizen in the Republic during his four years of office, and was designed with a view to residential comfort rather than State ceremonials. It was planned by an Irish architect, and is said to have been modelled after the Duke of Leinster's house in Dublin, itself an imitation of an Italian villa. The foundation stone was laid in 1792, John Adams, the next president in succession to George Washington, being the first occupant. He began to live there in 1800. In August, 1814, it was burnt by the British troops ; and in 1818 it was restored and re-occupied, and probably from this event dates the popular name, the White House, which has so universally replaced the official title of Executive Mansion. The chief apartments are on the ground floor, and consist of the East Room, eighty feet long and forty wide, the Blue, Red, and Green Rooms, forming a fine suite for reception rooms, and the State Dining Room. The Cabinet Room

THE WHITE HOUSE—MAIN ENTRANCE.

is a small apartment upon the first floor. In recent years the chief apartments have been very richly and tastefully decorated and furnished.

A very large amount of history has inseparably linked itself to the White House during the first century of its existence. Twenty-two presidents have resided there, four of whom succeeded from the vice-presidency because of the death of the president. Two chief magistrates of the nation, General W. H. Harrison in 1841, and General Zachary Taylor in 1849, died there. One, in many respects the greatest of the whole series, left the Red Room for a few hours' recreation, and was brought back amidst a nation's tears, the victim of a cruel and cowardly murder. Another was borne up the stairs of the southern entrance wounded by the shot of a disappointed scoundrel, to bear suffering heroically for long and weary weeks; finally to die at Long Branch. The outward history of what has been done in the White House is written in the annals of the nation; but no full record can ever appear of the joy and sorrow of family life, the play of mind upon mind, the conflict of opposing forces, the secret meetings, the undercurrent of intrigue, the constant revelation of much that is worst in human nature of which the White House has been the centre. While living here Buchanan allowed himself to be made the tool of Jefferson Davis and the men who forced upon the nation the Civil War. Here Abraham Lincoln, through those four awful years of struggle and bloodshed, spent his brain and heart and life in the service of the nation. Here he was besieged

THE REAR OF THE WHITE HOUSE.

by the endless hordes of rapacious office-seekers who were allowed to afflict the chief magistrate of the Republic in a way tolerated nowhere else under the sun. Here he lived through the anxieties of his first inauguration, of the outbreak of the rebellion, of the disasters of 1861 and 1862, of the critical Gettysburg campaign, of the closing scenes of the war. And here, amid all his public burdens and weighty responsibilities, he lived a quiet family life, finding in the society of his children refreshment of spirit and relief from the constant strain of an executive responsibility greater far than that borne by any other of its inhabitants. One who knew him intimately, and whose sources of information were quite exceptional, thus describes his life here :—

'During the first year of the administration the house was made lively by the games and pranks of Mr. Lincoln's two younger children, William

LINCOLN AND HIS SON AT THE WHITE HOUSE

and Thomas. The two little boys, aged eight and ten, with their Western independence and enterprise, kept the house in an uproar. They drove their tutor wild with their good-natured disobedience; they organised a minstrel show in the attic; they made acquaintance with the office-seekers, and became the hot champions of the distressed. William was a child of great promise, capable of close application and study. He had a fancy for drawing up railway time-tables, and would conduct an imaginary train from Chicago to New York with perfect precision. But this bright, gentle, studious child died in February, 1862. His father was profoundly moved by his death, though he gave no outward sign of his trouble, but kept about his work the same as ever. His bereaved heart seemed afterwards to pour out

THE CABINET ROOM, WHITE HOUSE.

its fulness on his youngest child. "Tad" was a merry, kindly little boy, perfectly lawless, and full of odd fancies and inventions, the "chartered libertine" of the Executive Mansion. He ran continually in and out of his father's cabinet, interrupting his gravest labours and conversations with his bright, rapid, and very imperfect speech—for he had an impediment which made his articulation almost unintelligible until he was grown. He would perch upon his father's knee, and sometimes even on his shoulder, while the most weighty conferences were going on. Sometimes escaping from the domestic authorities, he would take refuge in that sanctuary for the whole evening, dropping to sleep at last on the floor, when the President would pick him up and carry him tenderly to bed.

'As time wore on and the war held its terrible course, upon no one of all those who lived through it was its effect more apparent than upon the President. He bore the sorrows of the nation in his own heart; he suffered deeply, not only from disappointments, from treachery, from hope deferred, from the open assaults of enemies, and from the sincere anger of discontented friends, but also from the world-wide distress and affliction which flowed from the great conflict in which he was engaged, and which he could not evade. One of the most tender of men, he was forced to give orders that cost thousands of lives; by nature a man of order and thrift, he saw the daily spectacle of unutterable waste and destruction which he could not prevent. The cry of the widow and the orphan was always in his ears; the awful responsibility resting upon him as the protector of an imperilled Republic kept him true to his duty, but could not make him unmindful of the intimate details of that vast sum of human misery involved in a civil war.'[1]

The White House is flanked by two enormous masses of building. The pile to the west, handsome and ornate, and built of granite, contains the chief executive departments, those of State, War, and Navy. Each Department contains very fine rooms, and all the needful appliances for the adequate despatch of public business. They are all open to the public daily. On the eastern side of the Executive Mansion rises the splendid Ionic building used as the United States Treasury, 468 feet long, 264 feet wide. It contains about 200 rooms, the finest being the Cash Room, which is two storeys high, and is lined with handsome marbles. The Gold Room, the silver vaults and the various printing departments are well worth a visit.

The mere enumeration of the many public offices and institutions in Washington would occupy far more space than we can give. We pass them all by but two, the Capitol and the Smithsonian Institute. The Capitol is the centre and shrine of the Federal Government. Here the President is inaugurated. Here the Senate and the House of Representatives hold their Sessions. Here the will of the people, as expressed at the polling booths, finds its ultimate expression. Here in reality the executive work of the administration receives its impulse and guidance.

And the building is worthy both of the duties and associations that centre here. Not a few are prepared to maintain that it is the finest public building in the world. The corner-stone was laid, under what is now the Law Library, on September 18, 1793, by George Washington. The original buildings were burned by the British troops in 1814; but they were speedily rebuilt, although it was not until 1827 that the edifice was completed. This earlier Capitol consisted of what is now only the central body of the great congeries of apartments, lobbies, committee rooms, legislative chambers, etc. The Rotunda was relatively small; the Senate met in what is now the home of the Supreme Court; the House of

---

[1] Colonel John Hay, in the *Century*, vol. xli. p. 35.

Representatives in what is now the Statuary gallery; and the Library had but a promise of the splendid collection which it now contains. It was in these older rooms that the great senators and representatives of the earlier age fought out their battles and established their reputations. It was in them that the voices of Daniel Webster, Calhoun, Clay, Randolph, Benton, Edward Everett, and of a host of others who did well their part in the legislative action of their time, were so often heard.

But by 1850 the building had become quite inadequate to the increasing

THE LIBRARY.

demands made upon it, and the suggestion that new and extensive wings should be added came from a member of the committee of public buildings, then of great note in the Senate, and later on destined to acquire a sinister reputation in a much larger arena, viz., Jefferson Davis. These immense additions are built of white marble, the old central block of building being painted white to harmonise with them. The north wing is given over to the Senate, the chamber of meeting containing accommodation for 120 members, and seating in the galleries 1000 spectators. The south wing is set apart for the House of Representatives with accommodation on the floor of its chamber for 400 members, and allotting comfortable space in the enormous galleries for 2000 spectators. The Republic does not permit her legislators to work in a corner, and it is seldom indeed that sufficient constituents are present to occupy more than a small part of the generous accommodation placed at their disposal. Both houses meet at noon, and are generally completing their day's work by the time the British House of Commons is well under way.

As a result of the addition of these enormous wings it was felt that a new and more imposing central dome should be added. This was not completed until after the Civil War. The whole of the enormous edifice is richly decorated, and both the old and the new legislative chambers are among the finest, if not actually the finest in the world.

The Capitol stands well upon the top of a hill 90 feet high. It covers an area of 3½ acres; the central pile being 352 feet long and 121 feet deep, while each of the wings measures 230 feet in length and 140 feet in depth. The main front is towards the east, and looks away from the city. This is said to be due to the fact that although the city was planned to be built upon the high ground in that direction, as soon as that site was

THE ROTUNDA IN THE CAPITOL.

definitely fixed upon for the national capital wealthy men purchased all the land and asked such exorbitant prices that most of those who needed residences preferred to build upon the swampy and less-desirable, but much cheaper land to the west. The east front is adorned with three grand porticoes with Corinthian columns. The Rotunda is 96 feet in diameter, and 186 feet high. Above this towers the dome, the ceiling of which is 220 feet from the floor. The exterior is crowned by a huge statue of Liberty, lifted up more than 300 feet above the base of the building. From a gallery at the top of the dome superb views are obtained over the city, the Potomac, and the surrounding country.

In this connection we must glance for a moment at the system of government centering in the Capitol—the Federal, as distinct from State

GENERAL SHERMAN.

government. In very many most important matters each State in the Union is a sovereign power, having its own capital and legislature, and making its own laws. But when in 1789 the Constitution of the Republic was formulated, it provided that certain judicial, legislative and administrative functions, of equal importance to all the States, and of a kind to be undertaken only by a central government, must be considered Federal matters, and be transacted at Washington. These naturally included such things as war and peace, treaties with foreign states, the army and navy, federal courts, commerce, currency, copyright and patents, post office, taxation for these purposes, and also for the administration needful to accomplish them.

Congress consists of two bodies—the House of Representatives and the Senate. Representatives must be inhabitants of the State for which they sit, and at least twenty-five years old. The term is two years, and hence each period of two years is termed a Congress. The Representatives are elected

SOLDIERS' GRAVES, ARLINGTON.

according to population, the large States, like New York and Pennsylvania, having numerous members. The number is constantly changing, but is now (1891) fast nearing 350. A senator must be at least thirty years old, and must have lived in the State he represents for at least nine years previous to his election. He is elected by the Legislature of his State. Each State, quite irrespective of size or population, sends two members to the Senate, so that in this powerful and important body Rhode Island has just as much influence as New York. Then the elections are so arranged that one-third of the Senate has to be re-elected every two years. Hence each senator holds his seat for six years, and it takes at least six years to wholly change the constitution of the house. This arrangement was designed in order to secure continuity in at least one House of Congress. Every bill must pass both Houses, and be signed by the President before becoming law. If the

I

President wishes to do so he can veto any bill. It then goes back to Congress, and then if passed by a two-thirds vote becomes law in spite of the Presidential veto. If the President retains a bill ten days without signing it, it becomes law, unless in the meantime Congress has adjourned. Hence all bills passed during the last ten days of any Congress are at the mercy of the President. All money bills originate in the House of Representatives.

The President must be a native of the United States, at least thirty-five years old. He is the executive head of the government, makes treaties, but these are valid only if sanctioned by a two-thirds vote in the Senate; appoints ambassadors, consuls, judges, etc., but his appointments have to be confirmed by the Senate; he is commander-in-chief of the army and navy; and the heads of the various departments of state are responsible to him. The cabinet consists of the heads of the following departments: state, treasury, war, navy, post office, interior, and of justice. None, however, of these great state officers have a seat in Congress; their duties are executive rather than legislative. The President receives £10,000 a year; the cabinet ministers £1,600.

LEE'S HOUSE, ARLINGTON.

The system of Federal Government is very far from being simple and easily grasped. It is in many of its most important details a complex system aiming at securing the balance of conflicting forces. An adequate sketch of it is quite beyond the limitations of space in this book. But any reader curious on the subject—and all interested in the government of the British Empire should care to know how the greatest rival system has worked and is working—will find that a few hours spent in the careful reading of Professor Bryce's *The American Commonwealth* will put him in possession of a large body of facts, all grouped and arranged in the way best suited for such a comparison.

Visitors to Washington addicted to scientific pursuits make a point of visiting the Smithsonian Institution, a very handsome red stone building standing in lovely grounds 52½ acres in extent. It was founded by James Smithson, an Englishman, 'for the increase and diffusion of knowledge among men.'

It contains a natural history museum, together with metallurgical, ethnographical and geological collections. Connected with it is the National Museum, in which are preserved in permanent form many of the exhibits of the Philadelphia Centennial Exhibition of 1876.

Before quitting the capital we must pay a flying visit to a few points of unusual beauty or peculiar historic interest. The Soldiers' Home is a cluster of buildings about three miles to the north of the Capitol, crowning a high plateau. They are surrounded by a park of 500 acres, and the drive out and through the park is well calculated to impress one with the great

THE HALL, MOUNT VERNON.

beauty of suburban Washington. This was a favourite resort of President Lincoln, and he often spent the night here. It is now used as a home for disabled soldiers of the regular army.

On the south bank of the Potomac, and also reached by a lovely drive, is another spot of great beauty and rich in association with the past, Arlington House, a fine example of an old Virginian country mansion. At the outbreak of the Civil War it was occupied by Robert E. Lee, who afterwards became so famous as the great Confederate general. From the slopes in front of the house superb views are obtained, embracing the winding Potomac, the broad streets and numerous public buildings of Washington, and the rolling hills which surround that city. During the war this property was confiscated, the extensive and delightful grounds being turned into a National Cemetery, and the house preserved as a place of public interest. Nearly 15,000 men who fell in the war are interred here. About twenty-five years after the confiscation the United States Government recouped the descendants of General Lee with a sum equal in value to the property thus appropriated for ever to national use.

Going back to an earlier epoch, and connected with the life of a still greater man, Mount Vernon, the home and the last resting-place of George Washington, is the shrine to which multitudes of pilgrims, American and foreign, resort every year. It is situated on the Potomac, fifteen miles below Washington, and is most pleasantly reached by steamer. It was bequeathed in 1743 to Lawrence Washington, the half-brother of George, and by him renamed after Admiral Vernon, under whom he had seen service. George inherited it in 1752. The central portion of the house was built by Lawrence, the wings were added by George. From this house Washington went forth to those Indian conflicts which first made his name famous. Hither he brought home his bride, the celebrated Martha Washington. Here during his early married life he planted many of the trees of which he was so fond, and constantly improved and developed the fine old garden. Hence he was summoned to act as Commander-in-chief of the Colonial troops. From this dearly-loved home in 1789 he left to enter upon his eight years' Presidency of the new republic; and hither in 1797 he returned to spend quietly and happily the closing months of his useful life. In a room of the old mansion he died in December 1799, and in the grounds he was buried in the tomb where he sleeps by the side of his wife. In 1856 the house and six acres of land were purchased and presented to the nation.

SENDING A CARD TO A
MEMBER OF CONGRESS.

IN THE REFRESHMENT
ROOM AT THE CAPITOL.

A COTTON FIELD.

CHAPTER V.

THE SOUTH.

THE cities and scenery of the Southern States, to say nothing of the very interesting social and political features which they present, deserve a much more extended treatment than we can give them. In them negro slavery attained such extent and power that nothing short of that vast national convulsion, civil war, could put an end to it. In them at the present day there are three classes of people with little, if anything, in common. There is the dominant white class, made up of the descendants of the old slave-holding planters, and a section of immigrants who since the war have added to the capital and the brains of the community.

There is the class of whites, the equivalent for the generation of the 'poor whites' of the earlier epoch. Then there are the negroes, from six to seven millions in number, for ever free from any and all the restraints of slavery. The Federal Government has bestowed upon them the political power conferred by the suffrage, and has only inadequately provided education for them. By a mixture of force, fraud, and the influence of a superior race, the negroes are practically excluded from all share in the government of the states in which they live.

The South is very sparsely peopled. It is, however, well known that parts of North Carolina, Georgia, Alabama and Tennessee are very rich in mineral wealth, such as iron, copper, and coal. Already manufactures are springing up, and towns like Birmingham in Alabama are growing with a rapidity akin to that shown in the Western States. In the course of time it is highly probable that the Southern States will become the centre of a very large population. The climate, verging as it does upon the tropical, is not without considerable influence upon the habits and thought of the people.

'STONEWALL' JACKSON.

All these things render a trip through the South a journey full of variety, freshness and instruction. It is also an easy journey, railway communication with New Orleans being very good. The completion of the Southern Pacific route has rendered it possible to pass through the South either going to or returning from the Pacific Coast.

As noted in the last chapter, Washington stands just within the limits of the Southern States. A railway journey of a few hours takes the traveller from the Federal capital to Richmond. The distance is only 116 miles, and there is nothing at all uncommon in the scenery. The railroad first follows the course of the Potomac, and then runs across the edge of a somewhat desolate district, which was the scene of some of the most sanguinary battles of the Civil War. The railroad crosses the Rappahannock at Fredericksburg, a little town notable only for the fact that here in December 1862 a battle was fought, conspicuous for the bad generalship of General Burnside, the splendid bravery of the Northern troops, the decisive victory of General Lee's army, and the terrible bloodshed during the conflict, no less than 12,500 being killed and wounded on the Union, and 5,000 on the Confederate side. About twelve miles to the west of Fredericksburg the battle of Chancellorsville was fought in May 1863. Here Hooker was defeated by Lee, but at the close of the battle the famous Confederate general, 'Stonewall' Jackson, was mortally wounded. He died on May 10, in the house of a friend at a place called Guinneys, about twelve miles south of Fredericksburg. In the country lying to the south and west of this little town the great hand-to-hand struggle between Lee and Grant was fought out in the summer of 1864, a struggle which resulted in fearful loss of life on both sides, but one which practically put an end to the hopes of the South.

As the train nears Richmond the country presents a more pleasing aspect. Efforts are now being made to develop all this region for residential purposes, and these efforts promise to be successful. Richmond itself, a town of about 70,000 inhabitants, is well situated along the northern bank of the James River, about 100 miles by water from Chesapeake Bay. The site of the town is hilly, and the surrounding country is possessed of much quiet beauty. The town is well laid out, and in the business section there are many fine buildings. Richmond will always be notable for the fact that it was the capital of the Confederate Government from 1861 to 1865; that for its capture the North put forth all its tremendous energies; and that with its fall came the immediate and total collapse of the rebellion.

It is now the centre of considerable manufacturing energy, and exports large quantities of tobacco and flour. In a central position, and upon the most prominent site in the city, stands the State Capitol, a good-sized building of no special architectural pretensions. In the centre of the building is a square hall surmounted by a dome, beneath which stands Houdon's noted statue of Washington. In the grounds of the State House is an equestrian statue of Washington by Crawford, supposed to be one of the finest bronzes in the world. Around the base stand statues of other Virginian worthies, the most notable being Patrick Henry and Thomas Jefferson. Among the many churches of the city special interest attaches to St. Paul's Episcopal, which stands at the corner of Grace and Ninth Streets. In it Jefferson Davis was worshipping on that April Sunday morning in 1865 when Lee's fateful telegram, announcing that his lines were broken, and that Richmond must be evacuated, was brought to him. The oldest church in the city is St. John's, a structure which dates from the pre-Revolutionary days, and which, like the old South Church in Boston, was often used in those stormy times for public meetings. Here in 1775 the Virginia Convention was held to decide upon the action of the colony, and here in 1788 the Convention was held which ratified the Constitution of the United States. It was in the former of these two assemblies that

STATUE OF WASHINGTON IN THE GROUNDS OF THE STATE HOUSE, RICHMOND.

Patrick Henry delivered that great speech which has afforded elocutionary practice to such myriads of juvenile Americans, at the close of which he delivered the famous peroration: 'It is in vain to extenuate the matter. Gentlemen may cry, Peace, peace; but there is no peace. The war is actually begun. The next gale that sweeps from the north will bring to our ears the clash of resounding arms. Our brethren are already in the field! Why stand we here idle? What is it that gentlemen wish? What would they have? Is life so dear, or peace so sweet, as to be purchased at the price of chains and slavery? Forbid it, Almighty God! I know not what course others may take; but as for me, give me liberty, or give me death.'

On the James River, from fifty to sixty miles below Richmond, is one of the most notable spots in the United States. There, at a place called

SITE OF THE FIRST SETTLEMENT IN VIRGINIA, 1607.

Jamestown, in honour of James I., the first permanent English settlement on the continent was made in 1607. The chief men concerned in this settlement were Bartholomew Gosnold, Edward Wingfield, and John Smith. The last-named, because of the widespread popularity of his books, which record the early history of the settlement, has come to be regarded as the moving spirit in the enterprise. There is little doubt that he was a bold, capable, energetic man, and Virginia owes him a debt of gratitude. There is also little doubt that he was not inclined to hide his light under a bushel, that he was a little too prone to speak against those in authority, and that he was accomplished in the art of adapting facts to the requirements of his personal history. Recent research compels us now to disbelieve the old story of our youth; how just as the descending club was about to dash out his brains, Pocahontas rushed forth, and by flinging herself upon him, arrested the club, touched the savage heart of her father, and saved Smith's life.   It

AN OLD VIRGINIAN MANSION.

is true Smith tells the story with touching detail in his *Generall Historie*, published in 1624, after Pocahontas had become famous; but he says nothing about it in his *True Relation* of 1608, and every other contemporary record dealing with Pocahontas is equally silent.

As we have already noted, much as America is indebted to the Virginian colonies, and important as the part played in history by her great men has been, it has been a good thing that the prevailing temper and influence of the country have come from New England.   The story of hardships bravely borne and ultimately rewarded is similar in both cases; but Virginia has never equalled Massachusetts in energy, wealth, develop-

THE NATURAL BRIDGE IN VIRGINIA.

ment, or influence upon the nation at large. The site of Jamestown was deserted ages ago, and the engraving on page 121 shows its present appearance. The ruined tower of the old church, the remains of a few tombs, alone mark the site where in 1607 Englishmen first effected a permanent lodgment upon the soil of the great western continent.

Virginia was the earliest

site of the old planter colonial life, and down to the Civil War remained one of the most representative centres of slave life. Its families represented the flower of the aristocracy of the Republic. It gave to the nation its first commander-in-chief and president; Thomas Jefferson and Henry Clay sprang from its soil. In it are still to be found, notwithstanding the terrible ravages of the four years during which it was the seat of civil war, some of the finest specimens of the old colonial mansion.

The western boundary of Virginia, separating it from the new State carved out of its territory during the Civil War, and called West Virginia, is formed by the ranges of the Alleghany Mountains. These mountains abound in very fine scenery, such as the traveller enjoys when traversing the Shenandoah Valley, or visiting the Peaks of Otter. The most noted spot is the great Natural Bridge, situated in Rockbridge County. A small stream, called Cedar Creek, here flows through a chasm between rocky walls about 200 feet high. At one point the abyss is spanned by an archway of rock. The span is nearly ninety feet, and the rock at the topmost point is forty feet thick. A public road passes over this great and useful feat of natural engineering. Many individuals have climbed the walls of the arch from the creek for the most objectionable purpose of cutting their names in the rock, to be an eyesore to succeeding visitors. It is sad to learn that even George Washington succumbed to this temptation, although, true to his nature, he cut it in a position higher than that attained by any former climber. In 1818 a foolhardy youth succeeded in climbing from the foot up to the top of the arch.

Even in Richmond the negroes are very numerous, and the further south one travels the more numerous they become. Here is one of the very serious problems with which the citizens of the United States have to deal. The Civil War once and for all put an end to the absurd and immoral theory—a theory defended by all but an insignificant minority of the ministers and people of the Southern Churches—that the negro belonged to an inferior race, and hence was divinely-ordained for servitude. Whether the gift of the suffrage was wise or foolish, he has it, and in all probability will continue to possess it. Moreover, while on the one hand few, if any, of the evils that were always described as certain to follow emancipation have occurred, on the other, many of the great blessings it was to bring yet await their realization. Yet the signs are on the whole favourable. It is true that being no longer forced to labour, multitudes will do only just enough work to enable them to live. But the fact that they work for their own living and for the support of their families is to that extent an education, and the productive labour power of the nation is being strengthened by a much healthier force than 'involuntary servitude' ever was. It is true, perhaps, that not more than fifty per cent. ever go to school, and that not more than ten per cent. can read well; but on the other hand educational advantages are slowly and surely advancing, and the facts are largely in favour of the view that negro children are very well able to use these profitably.

Perhaps the feature of American treatment of the negro most objectionable to a European is the social ban under which they live. No one would advocate intermarriage. The evil results of intercourse between the white and the negro were only too apparent in the old slavery days. But it strikes the European as somewhat near a violation of the statements of the Declaration of Independence upon the equality of all men to prevent the

A NEGRO VILLAGE IN ALABAMA.

negro from using public conveyances, from staying at hotels, from sitting in the same part of public buildings, and from using the same schools as the whites simply because of his race peculiarity. Even where the law gives him certain rights it is often next to impossible to get the law to act on his behalf when invoked. Nevertheless, after making full allowance for all these things, one feels sure that time and the good sense of the American people will ultimately settle the right and just relations of the negro to the rest of the community.

A trip through the South enables the traveller to see also the brighter and livelier sides of the negro life and character. A great part of the work connected with the cotton crop is still done by them. The religious peculiarities familiar to all who have lived near a negro settlement, or who have read *Dred* or *Uncle Tom's Cabin*, are still prominent. The negro fondness for dress and display is often shown in a way very amusing to the onlooker.

The great product of the South now, as in the old slavery days, is cotton. The fear that free labour would limit the production of this all-important commodity has been dissipated by experience. During the last years of the old system the average annual crop was about 3,000,000 bales ; under free labour it has risen to over 4,000,000 bales. In 1879, the yield was nearly 6,000,000 bales. Rice, sugar, and tobacco are also very extensively grown, and some parts of the Far South are great fruit-growing districts.

It is impossible for us to linger, as we should like, at Charleston, where in 1861 the first shot of the war was fired ; at Montgomery, where the provisional Confederate Government was organized ; at some of the new centres of manufacture and commerce in Georgia and Alabama, or at some of the health-giving seaside resorts of Florida. And we can give but a passing glance at the great port of the Southern States seated near the mouth of the mighty Mississippi, the ' Father of Waters,' New Orleans. Settled in the course of the first half of the eighteenth century, held first by the French, then by Spain and again by the French, it was finally ceded with the whole province of Louisiana to the United States in 1803. Twice it has figured prominently in modern warfare. In 1815, Andrew Jackson defeated a British expedition sent to effect its capture ; and early in 1862 its capture by Farragut was one of the first great successes of the North in the Civil War. It has grown very rapidly in population, and also, as it was certain to do from its site, as a great centre of shipping trade. In 1810 it numbered only 17,243 inhabitants ; in 1890, 246,000. Through it the great bulk of the cotton crop passes to England and other parts of the globe, and its export trade amounts to about £30,000,000 annually.

It is well laid out and spacious, having many thoroughfares. The chief among the public buildings are the Custom House, the Mint, the City Hall, and the Roman Catholic Cathedral of St. Louis. The two sights most full of interest to the stranger are the French Market and the Levee. The New Orleans of to-day is the result of a more complex mixture of influences due to race, religion and climate than obtains anywhere else in the Republic. The old French and Spanish adventurers, the English settler, the negro, the modern American have all representatives in the people of to-day. The atmosphere, the tone, the point of view, is French rather than American, and the older and most picturesque part of the city is essentially French.

The war experiences came upon it as a severe discipline. It suffered, and to some extent out of its suffering it came ennobled and purified. In the city, which was once the hotbed of secessionist and proslavery schools, there are now admirable schools for the education of the negro. A keen observer writes : 'One might make various studies of New Orleans ; its commercial life ; its methods, more or less antiquated, of doing business, and the leisure for talk that enters into it ; its admirable charities, and its mediæval prisons ; its romantic French and Spanish history, still lingering in the old houses, and traits of family and street life ; the city politics,

From Harper's Magazine. Copyright by Harper & Brothers.

THE LEVEE AT NEW ORLEANS.

which nobody can explain and no other city need covet ; its sanitary condition, which needs an intelligent despot with plenty of money and an ingenuity that can make water run up hill ; its coloured population—about one-fourth of the city ; its schools and libraries ; its cuisine, peculiar in its mingling of French and African skill, and determined largely by a market unexcelled in the quality of fish, game and fruit ; the climatic influence in assimilating races meeting there from every region of the earth. But in whatever way we regard New Orleans, it is in its aspect, social tone, and character *sui generis*; its civilisation differing widely from that of any other, and it remains one of the most interesting places in the Republic.'

The great river upon which it lies is at once its making and its danger. The great levee is formed by the embankment which is needful to prevent the river in flood from sweeping the whole city away. There are no storage cellars there, because no place below ground is dry enough for constant use. And on the levee, where the foreign steamers take in their enormous cargoes of cotton, sugar, rice and tobacco; where the great river steamboats lade for their journey of one or two thousand miles up the mighty stream; where congregate the various classes of the motley population, from the negro labourer up to the wealthy citizen, there are perhaps more scenes calculated to arouse the interest and stimulate the curiosity of the observer than can be witnessed in any similar locality in the whole United States.

STREET LIFE IN THE SOUTH.

K

NIAGARA : THE AMERICAN FALL FROM GOAT ISLAND.

THE WHIRLPOOL RAPIDS, NIAGARA FALLS.

CHAPTER VI.

TO CHICAGO VIÂ NIAGARA.

OF the two great routes to the West the preference, so far as scenic beauty is concerned, must be given to that taken by the New York Central Railway. This hugs the eastern bank of the Hudson as far as Albany, and then crosses New York State, enabling the traveller to see the lovely valley of the Mohawk and the wonders of Niagara. The continuance of the westward journey brings the great lakes within our ken, and terminates at Chicago. We propose in the present chapter to pass rapidly over this journey of more than 900 miles.

The New York starting-point is the handsome and imposing station known as the Grand Central Depot in 42nd Street. If time allows, the pleasantest way of taking the first stage of the journey is to go to Albany by the Hudson River day boat, which takes about nine hours for the trip. In this way the ever-varying beauties of the Hudson may be seen to the greatest advantage, and most thoroughly

enjoyed.   But although the views obtained from the train are less extensive
and more rapid, to the lover of natural beauty they furnish from four to
five hours of continuous delight.   As soon as the northern outskirts of New

THE GRAND CENTRAL DEPOT, NEW YORK.

York are reached, the rocky precipices of the Palisades appear on the western
bank.   They often reach a height of 300 feet, and extend for fifteen miles.
The train runs rapidly past Tarrytown, the scene of many revolutionary
incidents and inseparably associated with the memory of Washington Irving;
past Sing Sing, the great prison, and Peekskill nestling in one of the great

bends of the river, and forming the portal of the Highlands. This is the centre of the loveliest scenery of the Hudson, and for sixteen miles ever-changing landscapes of extreme beauty charm the eye. Here are Dunder-berg and Anthony's Nose and Sugar-loaf Mountains; and a few miles higher up is West Point, the seat of the National Military Academy, where Grant and Sherman, and Lee and Jackson, and a host of other generals who served in the Civil War, were educated, and where the young military cadets are still put through a severe but valuable course of training. Above West Point are Cro' Nest and Storm King, two of the most noted of the Highlands. The scenery north of these becomes somewhat tame in comparison, yet it everywhere presents features which charm and delight. Poughkeepsie, seventy-five miles from New York, lies in a lovely situation, and is the centre of many important educational institutions, the chief among them being Vassar College, one of the most noted colleges for girls in the world. Further north, on the western bank, are the Catskill Mountains, and just as Albany is reached the train crosses the river by a bridge.

THE LAST MOMENT ON THE RAILWAY POST OFFICE.

Journeys of this kind exhibit the many superior advantages on the side of American as contrasted with English railway carriages. Even from an ordinary car the view is much more extensive and more easily enjoyed; but these advantages are greatly increased if the views are seen through the wide plate-glass windows and from a comfortable armchair in a luxurious Wagner Palace car. The American system is also unquestionably the better for the long journeys, extending as they often do over three, four, or five days and nights; but on the other hand the average speed in the United States is considerably below that reached by all the great British main lines. It is, however, a great comfort to be able to move about whenever you feel disposed, and from the platform of the carriage many special objects can be well seen. In the many little devices for comfort and convenience the

Americans are far ahead of the English. The American conductor is much more accessible, and can be rendered much more useful than the English guard ; and conveniences like that shown in the engraving on page 133 are not to be despised. The permanent way is now much better made than it used to be, and on the trunk lines a high rate of speed is attainable with perfect safety. The absence of bridges and fences and the consequent frequency of level crossings render necessary the constant use of the hoarse steam whistle. It is in the matter of stations, or depots as they are universally called in America, that things seem often very rough to an English eye.

THE CONDUCTOR.

Platforms are almost unknown, and in many of the wayside stations accommodation for the travelling public is of a very scanty order. In a large number of them the absence of creature comfort adds considerably to the inconvenience of those compelled to wait for a train, which on the long journeys may sometimes be an hour or two behind time.

Albany was originally settled by the Dutch in 1614 ; it was then called Fort Orange, and is contemporary with the original settlement upon Manhattan Island. In 1664 it was named Albany, after the Duke of York and Albany, better known in history as James II. of England ; and in 1798 it became the capital of the State of New York. From the advantages of the site it was certain to become a place of commercial importance, standing as it does at the head of the navigable waters of the Hudson, and being the point to which come the great Erie Canal from Buffalo in the West, and the Champlain Canal from the north. It is also a great railway centre. As the eye ranges over the city when it first comes into view it rests upon many fine buildings and churches, the most important being the Capitol, in which the Legislature holds its sessions, and the City Hall. The former is an imposing edifice of Maine granite, 400 feet wide and 300 feet deep, with

A WAYSIDE RAILWAY DEPOT.

a tower 320 feet high; of the latter we give a view in the engraving on page 137.

In this connection a word or two upon State as distinct from Federal Government may not be out of place. Every State in the Union has an executive elective head called the governor, other necessary administrative officers, a Legislature of two houses, and a system of courts of justice. All amendments of the State Constitution are submitted to the direct vote of the people, who also elect the governor and chief officials. These never have a seat in the Legislature. Each State has its own peculiarities in regard to its constitution and administration, but in the following respects all are alike. Each Legislature consists of a Senate and a House of Represen tatives. Those States which tried the experiment of having only one house have all abandoned it, the theory and experience being, apparently, that only by means of two houses can the needful check to hasty and corrupt legislation be secured. The members of both houses are chosen by direct popular vote, the district represented by a senator being usually twice or thrice as large as that for which a representative sits. The term of a senator is generally longer than for a representative. Universal suffrage is the rule, crime, including bribery, in all, and receipt of poor law relief in a few States alone disqualifying the voter. The numbers in the Legislature necessarily vary with the size of the State and the area of its elective districts. In some cases the Senate has only ten or a dozen members, in others fifty; the House of Representatives is, in Delaware twenty-one, in Massachusetts two hundred and forty. In all the States the members are paid, the annual sum varying from £30 to £300; taking the average of all the States the value of a legislator is about £100 a year. In some States this public service is appraised at a certain daily sum for the period of the session. Thus Rhode Island pays her legislators four shillings, California thirty shillings a day. It is hardly needful to remark that where this system prevails the length of the session is fixed by statute; Oregon, for example, thinking forty days sufficient for the business to which Pennsylvania gives one hundred and fifty. In the great majority of the States the sessions are biennial, a result due in most cases to the hasty and over-legislation of the past, and also to the fact that political corruption finds its most profitable field in the State Legislatures. In the great majority of States a governor may veto any bill, but it may be passed over his veto by majorities ranging from an actual to one of two-thirds. The power of the Legislature is in all of the States limited by various constitutional enactments. Certain subjects are expressly excluded from the jurisdiction of the Legislature; such, for example, as granting titles, endowing religion, permitting lotteries, increasing the debt beyond a fixed amount, etc. In many cases the constitution fixes the majority necessary to pass bills, and the method of taking the votes of members forbids rushing bills at the end of a session.

As to the general condition of State Legislatures in the United States with regard to political purity, and the peculiar reputation of the one which meets at Albany, we cannot do better than quote Professor Bryce:—

'It is hard to form a general judgment regarding the State Legislatures, because they differ so much among themselves. Those of Massachusetts, Vermont, and several of the North-western States, such as Michigan, are pure, i.e., the members who would take a bribe are excessively few, and those who would push through a job for some other sort of consideration a small fraction of the whole. On the other hand, New York and Pennsylvania have so bad a name that people profess to be surprised when a good act passes, and a strong governor is kept constantly at work vetoing bills

THE CITY HALL, ALBANY.

corruptly obtained, or mischievous in themselves. Several causes have contributed to degrade the Legislature of New York State. It is comparatively small in number, the Assembly having but 128 members, the Senate

32. It includes, beside New York and Brooklyn, several smaller ring-governed cities whence bad members come. It has to deal with immensely powerful corporations, such as the great railroads which traverse it on their way to the west; these corporations are the bane of state politics, for their management is secret, being usually in the hands of one or two capitalists, and their wealth is so great that they can offer bribes at which ordinary virtue grows pale. There are many honest men in the Assembly, and a few are rich men who do not need a *douceur*, but the proportion of tainted men is large enough to pollute the whole lump. Of what the bribe-taker gets he keeps a part for himself, using the rest to buy the doubtful votes of purchaseable people; to others he promises his assistance when they need it, and when by such log-rolling he has secured a considerable backing, he goes to the honest men, among whom, of course, he has a considerable acquaintance, puts the matter to them in a plausible way—they are probably plain farmers from the rural districts—and so gains his majority. Each great corporation keeps an agent at Albany, the capital of the State, who has authority to buy off the promoters of hostile bills, and to employ the requisite lobbyists. Such a lobbyist, who may or may not be himself a member, bargains for a sum down, $5,000 or $10,000 (£1,000 or £2,000), in case he succeeds in getting the bill in question passed or defeated as the case may be; and when the session ends he comes for his money, and no questions are asked. This sort of thing now goes on, or has lately gone on in several other States, though nowhere on so grand a scale. Virginia, Maryland, California, Illinois, Missouri are all more or less impure; Louisiana is said to be now worse than New York.'[1]

After leaving Albany the train runs nearly due west through the whole breadth of New York State, traversing the lovely Mohawk Valley and passing through Syracuse and Rochester to Buffalo, the important town situated at the eastern extremity of Lake Erie. Buffalo is a great centre of canal traffic, grain transport, and iron works. But for the ordinary traveller its chief attraction is the fact that it forms a starting-point for the excursion to Niagara Falls, the natural marvel which ranks with the Yosemite Valley and the Yellowstone Park, and which in many respects is even more impressive than either of its great rivals, while the ready access to Niagara greatly increases its popularity.

The stupendous falls which constitute Niagara occur on the river of that name thirty-six miles in length, through which the waters of Lake Erie flow into Lake Ontario. The falls occur about twenty-two miles below Lake Erie, and the best general view of them is obtained from either the suspension or the railway bridge, some distance lower down the river. It is often stated that the first view is disappointing; if it be so, and this is by no means certain, it must be due to the fact that an incorrect impression has

[1] *The American Commonwealth*, vol. ii., p. 519.

been formed about the height of the falls. This is only 164 feet on the American, and 158 on the Canadian side; but the extent of the mighty resist-less onrush of the waters is gigantic. The edge over which the waters so madly plunge is 4,750 feet in width, and Goat Island, which separates the American from the Canadian fall, occupies about a quarter of the space. The American fall is 1,100 feet wide; the Canadian or Horseshoe Fall about 2,200 feet. The enormous breadth of the falling water greatly heightens the charm and impressiveness of Niagara. It has pleased some

HENNEPIN'S SKETCH OF NIAGARA IN 1678.

scientists to make rough calculations as to the amount of water that passes over every minute, but the figures are too large to convey any definite idea to the mind. Perhaps the best method of comprehending the stupendous scale of this natural marvel is to remember that it is the sole outlet for the water of four great inland seas lying hundreds of feet above the level of the ocean: Lake Superior, 355 miles long and 160 miles wide; Lake Michigan, 320 miles long and 70 wide; Lake Huron, 260 miles long and 100 wide; and Lake Erie, 290 miles long and 65 wide. It is from these inexhaustible sources that the mighty streams, ever passing, ever abiding in views of glorious beauty, have come age after age, and will probably continue to come for thousands and thousands of years.

We give an engraving of the first known view of the falls taken from Father Hennepin's description, written in 1678. We give also a little of his verbal description : ' Betwixt the Lake Ontario and Erie there is a vast and prodigious cadence of water which falls down after a surprising and astonishing manner, insomuch that the universe does not afford its parallel. This wonderful downfall is compounded of two cross-streams of water and two falls, with an isle sloping along the middle of it. The waters which fall from this horrible precipice do foam and boil after the most hideous manner imaginable, making an outrageous noise, more terrible than that of thunder; for when the wind blows out of the south their dismal roaring may be heard more than fifteen leagues off.'

Rough and careless in detail as Hennepin's sketch is in all probability, it serves a useful purpose in giving us some measure of the changes of the last 200 years. In his engraving there is no sign of the two falls on the American side, the centre of the Canadian fall had not been eaten away, and there was a third fall which rushed over by the side of Table Rock. This fall has since been drained by the retrogression of the cataract, and the last fragment of Table Rock fell in 1850. Facts like these are conclusive that the falls are rapidly changing. Within the last fifty or sixty years they have receded about 100 feet on the Canadian side. Geologists are of opinion that the waters have cut their way through the whole length of the gorge from Lewiston, a distance of seven miles. The present rate of excavation is variously estimated from an inch to a foot a year. Assuming it to be the latter, the line of the falls can hardly change in any very appreciable degree during the next few centuries.

In former years the enjoyment of a visit to Niagara was greatly marred by the various vexatious charges which had to be paid for access to any point of special interest, and many unsightly buildings interrupted some of the best views. In 1885 the State of New York purchased all the property bordering upon the falls, and has laid it out to the best possible advantage as a national pleasure ground under the name Niagara Park. In like manner the Canadian Government has acquired and laid out for public use the land on their side of the falls. The result is that the visitor can now wander at will about both sides of the river, and enjoy to his mind's content the views and objects that most fascinate and delight him.

By a happy accident a number of rocky islets, to which access is gained by bridges, lie out in the rapids on the American side of the river, and some of them are on the very verge of the falls. These present many magnificent points of view from which to study the mighty masses of falling water, or, what to most minds is still more impressive and awe-inspiring, the terrific onrush of the waters in the rapids just before they take the fearful plunge.

From Niagara Park a superb view of the American Fall is obtained, the parapet at Prospect Point affording a front view of the fall and coming so close to the water that you can almost touch it with the hand as it rushes down. A short distance above this fall the rapid leading to it is crossed by a bridge which rests first upon Bath Island, and then extends over a narrower rapid to Goat Island. The total length of the bridge is 360 feet, and it is not easy at first to shake off the sense of painful insecurity as you lean over the slender railing, and watch the water gliding beneath your feet with awful velocity and resistless might. The view up the rapids from this bridge is usually one of the first, and one of the most abiding impressions which the 'Thunder of Waters' makes upon the visitor.

Upon reaching Goat Island, which has an area of about sixty acres, a path leads down to the inner edge of the American Fall, and thence a bridge spans what is known as Centre Fall, and gives access to Luna Island, a huge mass of rock placed on the very edge of the falls, and affording another superb point of vantage from whence to study the American Fall.

Upon Goat Island, Biddle's Stairs, as they are called, enable those who are courageous enough to do so, and who care to go to the trouble and expense of donning a special suit of waterproof clothing, to pass out upon the rocks right across the face of Centre Fall, and then, coming in to the rock between Centre Fall and the American Fall, to pass under the Centre Fall, and so regain the starting-point. It is a perfectly safe journey, and the writer had no difficulty in making it in the company of a lady and a gentleman and a guide; and certainly the impressions gained are unusual and full of abiding interest. To stand, as you do, well out in front of the mighty cataract, which seems to pour down from the skies, with the awful thunder of the whole of the falls in your ears, rendering any communications with your companions almost impossible, the spray driving so swiftly and strongly towards you that it is nearly impossible to face it and the vast column of water apparently bent upon sweeping you away before it, is both novel and exhilarating. Then as you turn in towards the rock troubles increase. Sight is nearly useless by reason of the driving spray, the rocks appear to present only a precarious footing, you can hardly catch the reassuring words of the guide that it is 'perfectly safe,' and when you finally get under the very Centre Fall itself, with the grim rock within and the awful mass of falling water without, and with the violent currents of wind created by the fall seemingly intent upon driving you out into the raging whirlpool beyond, your sensations are apt to be more lively than pleasure-able. Nevertheless there is something very stimulating in thus standing, if it be only for a moment, in the very centre and vortex of one of the world's greatest wonders.

For those who have the nerve to see them, and who are favoured by suitable atmospheric conditions, this trip often affords wonderful rainbow effects. But from certain points of view, when the sun is shining, there are always rainbows visible at Niagara, and most prefer to enjoy them from quieter and drier standpoints.

At the opposite end of Goat Island, and stretching right out into the midst of the rapids leading to the Canadian Fall, are three tiny rocky islets known as the Three Sisters. These are connected by bridges, and from the outermost a magnificent view of the great rapids is obtained. It is difficult to convey any adequate conception of the grandeur of the scene at this point. You sit upon a rock raised only a foot or two above the water; at your feet it is almost still, conflicting currents reducing it to a state approaching equilibrium, and yet only a yard or two away it is rushing onward with a roar that fills the ear, and a force that impresses the mind with the utter helplessness of man or beast or boat luckless enough to get caught in that awful current.

Here also the enormous breadth of the river and the rapid slope towards the gigantic Horseshoe Fall heighten the interest of the scene. As you sit upon the verge of the outermost of the Three Sisters and look up the stream, the waters appear to be rolling down upon you with a might that nothing can restrain, to sweep both you and the islet away to the dreadful fall just below. And then at the very instant when destruction seems inevitable, they part and rush by on either side, too intent upon reaching the fall to stay and sweep away so slight an obstacle as the rock on which you sit. After repeated study of the falls and rapids, the writer's conviction is that the experience which combines best the impressions of awe, of force, of destiny, and of a curious peace produced by the ever-changing, and yet ever-present forms of rushing water are nowhere quite so vivid and quite so memorable as upon that last and outermost rocky point in the midst of the Canadian rapid.

Goat Island stretches out towards the Canadian shore on what is known as Terrapin Rock, and this affords a very fine point from which to study the great Horseshoe Fall. This, as already noted, greatly exceeds the American Fall in size, being about double the width, but not so high by about six feet. From the greater force of the bigger mass of water, and also from the nature of the rock, the centre of the fall is receding much faster than the sides, and is being eaten out into a horseshoe shape. From a point on the Canadian shore a view is obtained into the very centre and heart of the cataract. The masses of green water, known to be at least twenty feet deep as they fall over the edge, and smooth with that fascinating smoothness always possessed by water about to pass into a cataract, fall over and inward, the outer sides of the horseshoe naturally turning towards the centre, and preserve their smooth, green, solid appearance for a few feet

THE FACE OF THE AMERICAN FALL IN WINTER.

below the edge, and then break into the wildest spray and send up to heaven their ceaseless thunders. Looking through a glass into this seething mass of waters, at times wholly obscured by clouds of spray, at others clear for an instant, and affording a view almost to the base of the fall, one could easily imagine it to be the home of the spirit of the waters, as inaccessible to living man, except by power of vision, as though situated in another sphere.

In winter the falls present a very different appearance. The spray gradually freezes, and in front of the American Fall forms ice bridges which enable the adventurous to obtain a nearer view than is possible anywhere except by the path in front of the Centre Fall.

A little steamer, the Maid of the Mist, moves about in perfect safety in the broad expanse of river just below the falls, and from her deck splendid views of the whole extent of Niagara are obtained. After the great plunge the waters act as though they were weary, and the breadth of the river is such that boating is comparatively safe. But about two miles below the falls the walls of the river contract, forming the Whirlpool Rapids, through which only one boat is known ever to have ridden in safety, and in trying to swim through which foolhardy persons have lost their lives. At the Whirlpool proper, an equally dangerous place, still lower down, the river makes an abrupt turn, and then the waters, after their ten miles of conflict and struggle, flow peacefully on into Lake Ontario.

Few experiences are more restful than a visit to Niagara. There, as at all 'scenic wonders of the world' frequented by the crowd, things exist that jar upon the mind of the sensitive. There is also a dread and terrible side to much of the scenery. Some come under the curious influence that seems to prompt them to leap into the rushing stream, and some points of view, like the inner edge of Luna Island, are too exacting for any but strong nerves. But on the whole the influence is uplifting and restful, and calculated to lift the thought up from the tremendous natural forces here in vigorous and beautiful exercise to Him who made them all, and in whose vision Niagara was beautiful myriads of years before there was a human eye to gaze upon its wonders, or a human heart to rejoice in the emotions it inspires.

There are several routes from Niagara to Chicago, none of which afford scenery of any exceptional merit. The great city itself, the centre of a growth in power and population phenomenal for speed even in the United States, stands on the western shore of Lake Michigan, near the southern end of that vast inland sea. The selection of the site was due to the fact that there the small stream known as the Chicago River empties into the lake. Permanent settlement began here in 1804, when Fort Dearborn was built. At the end of 1830 Chicago consisted of fifteen houses and about one hundred inhabitants. Its incorporation dates from 1837, and the census of that year, taken on July 1, showed a population of 4,170. In 1850 this had become 29,963; in 1860, 112,172; in 1870, 298,977; in 1880, 503,304; and in 1890, 1,100,000. This means that in the last ten years the great city has more than doubled the number of her citizens.

Meanwhile the boundaries of the city have been extending side by side with her growth in numbers. Originally the houses were grouped around the Chicago River, a bayou about half a mile long with branches known as

North and South running parallel to the lake for a distance of two miles. These streams divide the city into north, south, and west divisions, and also give, by means of slips and exclusive of the lake, a water frontage of about thirty miles. The different sections of the city are connected by numerous bridges and several tunnels. The area now embraced within the city limits extends nearly twenty-five miles north and south along the lake, and about fourteen miles inland in a westerly direction, in all about one hundred and seventy-five square miles. Around the whole southern end of the lake stretches for hundreds of miles the Illinois prairie, and the site of Chicago and the surrounding country is nearly a dead level. Fortunately there is a slight rise towards the west, thus rendering it easier to drain the city. The business portion of the city is now about fourteen feet above the lake, having been built up from three to nine feet since 1856.

The chief events in the history of Chicago so far have been the great Republican Convention, which, in 1860, nominated Abraham Lincoln as candidate for the Presidency; and the great fire in October, 1871. Built, as all these western towns so largely are, of wood, it was inevitable that a fire once well started would be most difficult to check. This conflagration began, it is supposed, by the upsetting of a kerosene lamp on the evening of Sunday, October 8. It raged all Monday, and did not burn itself out until Tuesday morning. By that time the houses over an area of three and a-half square miles, 17,450 in number, had been consumed; about 200 persons had been killed, and 98,500 rendered homeless. The loss was estimated at about £38,000,000, of which about £6,000,000 was recovered from insurance companies, most of which were reduced to bankruptcy.[1] The wide-spread sympathy which the calamity aroused, both in America and Europe, resulted in speedy help for the sufferers. The city showed a wonderful power of recovery, and to-day Chicago has many a street of handsome buildings which she would probably not possess had not the fire remorselessly swept away the earlier and poorer structures. A second but much less destructive fire ravaged part of the city in July 1874.

We give as a specimen of the recent architectural development of Chicago an engraving of the great Auditorium building. This stands upon a splendid site in Michigan Avenue overlooking the lake; it has a total street frontage of 710 feet, and is built externally of granite and Bedford stone. The main building is ten storeys high, and the tower rises another eight, and this is crowned by a lantern tower thirty feet high. The entire elevation from the ground to the top of the lantern is 270 feet. The cost has been £640,000, and it was begun in January 1887, and completed in February 1890. The block of building contains: first, the Auditorium, capable of holding 8,000 persons, with 'the most complete and costly stage

---

[1] The Liverpool and London and Globe Insurance Company of England were a remarkable exception. They paid £500,000 in immediate drafts, and gained enormous reputation, and increase of American business.

and organ in the world;' second, a Recital Hall, which will hold 500; third, the business portion, consisting of large shops on the ground floor, and 136 offices, part of which are in the tower; fourth, an observatory in the tower connected with the United States signal service; fifth, the Auditorium Hotel. This contains 400 rooms, and is most magnificently furnished and equipped. From the top of the tower, reached by a comfortable lift, a very extensive view over the city is obtained.

Chicago is now laid out in the rectangular method common to so many

THE AUDITORIUM BUILDING, CHICAGO.

large American cities. State, Clark, and Madison Streets are the chief centres of business. Chicago ranks second only to New York as a business centre, and ever since 1854 it has been the metropolis of the enormous western grain trade. The gigantic elevators for the storage and shipping of grain are one of the sights of the city. It possesses also a gigantic live stock trade, the great stock yards and pig-killing establishments being on a scale unapproached elsewhere in the world. The volume of Chicago trade is now between £200,000,000 and £300,000,000 every year.

Chicago has become the greatest railway centre on the American

continent. Long before the train reaches the city depot the evidences of
this are obvious in the miles and miles of freight trains that occupy the
multitudinous sidings. In the United States freight is carried almost if not
quite universally in large covered cars, and not, as so often in England, in

HARD TIMES ON A FREIGHT TRAIN.

open trucks. These trains often contain forty or fifty cars, and are drawn
by powerful engines; and seen on the grand scale, as in the outskirts of
Chicago, they convey a very lively impression of the grand scale on which
the inland trade of America is conducted. But this peculiarity of car

L 2

construction throws considerable hardship upon the men who have to manage the brakes. In passenger trains, for the most part, the brake power is applied directly from the engine by the use of the vacuum brake, a system not only more rapid, but much more efficacious than any of the old methods. But it has not yet been possible to apply this or any analogous system to freight trains, and in these the brakesmen have to run along the top of the cars applying the brake by hand. This may not be unpleasant on a fine summer day; but the work often has to be done under the conditions shown in the engraving on page 147, when the exposure must necessarily be great, and the risks of injury to limb and life not small.

Chicago occupies a magnificent position both as a railroad and business centre. Whether it will ever become the supreme city of the continent, as many of its admirers believe, time only can show. But, in any case, all travellers who wish to form correct impressions of the commercial power of the country should extend their westward wanderings at least as far as the great metropolis of the West.

A PULLMAN CAR PORTER.

The Cathedral Spires in the Garden of the Gods.

THE GRIZZLY BEAR.

CHAPTER VII.

To San Francisco viâ Denver and Salt Lake City.

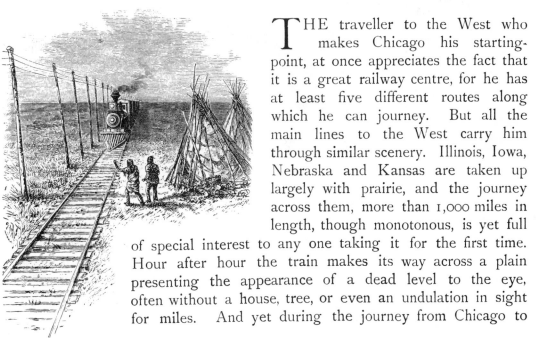

THE traveller to the West who makes Chicago his starting-point, at once appreciates the fact that it is a great railway centre, for he has at least five different routes along which he can journey. But all the main lines to the West carry him through similar scenery. Illinois, Iowa, Nebraska and Kansas are taken up largely with prairie, and the journey across them, more than 1,000 miles in length, though monotonous, is yet full of special interest to any one taking it for the first time. Hour after hour the train makes its way across a plain presenting the appearance of a dead level to the eye, often without a house, tree, or even an undulation in sight for miles. And yet during the journey from Chicago to

Denver the train really rises about 5,000 feet, but the slope is so gradual as to be scarcely perceptible at any point in the journey.

The route taken by the Chicago, Burlington and Quincy Railroad runs across the northern part of Illinois, spans the great Mississippi river at Burlington, affording a very fine view of the 'Father of Waters,' then traverses

A PULLMAN DINING CAR.

the entire length of Iowa in a line running nearly due east and west, and crosses the Missouri at Pacific Junction, only a short distance to the south of Council Bluffs and Omaha. Then the train passes in a south-westerly direction across the whole of Nebraska. Sitting comfortably in a Pullman car, either a palace sleeper, or, as occasion demands, in the well-appointed dining car, the eye ranges over an apparently limitless space of prairie.

The impression produced is exactly that of being at sea, only instead of ploughing one's way through the yielding and shifting water, one skims the surface of the solid but level land. Signs of population occur in the constant succession of little farmsteads which dot the landscape here and there. Almost all of them are built of wood, generally painted white, sometimes of a red or a chocolate colour, and nearly every one is provided with a small windmill for the purpose of pumping water. In this way the breezes which constantly sweep the prairie are turned to a very practical use. Where the fields are separated, it is usually done by a wire fencing, furnished with sharp-pointed spikes for the purpose of preventing the cattle from destroying them—a serviceable but a somewhat cruel device. Everywhere a country in the process of being settled passes under the eye. This effect is heightened every now and then by the sight of a 'prairie schooner,' that is, an emigrant party crossing the prairie in wagons, carrying with them their families and possessions, and taking several weeks to make the journey accomplished by the luxurious train in twenty-four hours.

After the boundary line of Colorado has been passed, every one is alert for the first view of the great mountain chain of the Rockies, which just to the west of Denver stretch like an impenetrable and impassable barrier across the continent. If seen under the light of an evening sun, with their huge, multitudinous, snow-covered peaks touched with the varied glories of a sunset glow, this view is one of the most impressive in all Nature. Denver is a town which owes much of its prosperity to geographical situation, just as Chicago seems to have been fore-ordained as the great railroad centre of the continent. Lying in the centre of a series of lofty plateaux which face towards the Rocky Mountains, the town seems destined by a certain and powerful natural selection to be the metropolis of the vast district embraced between the Mississippi and the Rocky Mountains. Few towns in the United States are more fortunate in site and situation. Stretching away north and south as far as the eye can range—and at this elevation, and in the clear atmosphere, the eye can range over a distance of at least a hundred and fifty miles north and south—are the giant summits of the great mountain chain. Pike's Peak, with its snow-white crown, seventy-five miles distant, glitters perfectly clear and sharp in the distant sky, and the great elevations of the chain slope towards the city, spread out in the great rolling lower masses known as the Foot Hills. These, in the clear, transparent atmosphere can be distinctly seen, and all their terraces traced; while the nearest of them, although apparently only an easy afternoon's walk away, are yet from twenty to thirty miles distant.

Like Chicago, only upon a much smaller scale, the growth of Denver has been exceedingly rapid. In 1837 a single hut occupied its site; in 1880 the population was 35,630; and in 1890, 115,000: that is, in the course of the last ten years the population has increased about 400 per cent. It is well laid out, but at the present time the vast majority of the inhabitants seem engrossed in the occupation of buying and selling land, which changes hands rapidly, and at an equally rapid increase of profit. What puzzles the stranger somewhat is where the money comes from to pay for these trans- actions, and how the people manage to live during their completion. Those not engaged in buying and selling land devote their attention to building, and the city is fast acquiring very handsome and very spacious buildings for public and for private use, and especially for business purposes. The streets are well laid out, but the inhabitants, apparently, have never found time to do more than fix the limits ; no attempt has yet been made to pave them properly, and consequently in summer the dust is exceedingly troublesome ; and in winter they are practically impassable. One pleasant feature is the system of irrigation, by which streams of water are kept running through the gutters, the object being thus to enable the trees planted along the side-walks to grow in this dry climate.

The finest route from Denver to the west is the Rio Grande Railroad, which, with a not altogether unjustifiable enthusiasm, is described by its proprietors as 'the scenic line of the world.' This runs first in a southerly direction, parallel to the great mountain chain, and at Colorado Springs and Manitou Springs possesses health resorts of a very high order. Colorado Springs lies out upon the plain, in full view of some of the highest peaks of the Rocky Mountains. Manitou Springs is nestled in among the foot- hills at the base of Pike's Peak. It is very well supplied with hotels, and is within reach of much lovely and unusual mountain scenery. From it, Pike's Peak, about 14,000 feet, can be easily ascended ; and now the summit can be attained by a railroad. The chief excursion of the district is to a place rejoicing in the somewhat exalted title of the 'Garden of the Gods.' This is a tract of country shut in by the mountains, and remarkable for the extraordinary forms which the red sandstone has assumed under stress of time and weather. To these weird and curious rocks all kinds of fanciful names are attached. The traveller is shown the Mushroom Garden, the Ant-eater, the Camels, the Lion, and a host of others, all more or less resembling the objects after which they are named. Perhaps the most interesting group is that known as the Cathedral Spires, of which we give an engraving on page 150. The portals to the garden are composed of huge masses of sandstone, and after entering a few hundred yards, on looking back these masses are seen to afford a superb natural frame for the enormous bulk of Pike's Peak, with its crown of everlasting snow, which towers aloft clear and sharp against the sky-line many miles away.

After leaving this district the train passes through Pueblo, the junction for Santa Fé, and then turns sharply to the west, and begins the great task of penetrating the vast mountain chain. To do this it has availed itself of the natural advantages afforded by two great rivers—the Arkansas, which rises on the western side of the Divide, and, after flowing over one thousand miles in an easterly direction, empties itself into the Mississippi ; and the Gunnison, which rises only a few miles from the Arkansas, but finally empties itself into

THE ROYAL GORGE OF THE ARKANSAS.

the Pacific, two thousand miles away. On this line, with its neighbouring branches, is found much of the finest mountain scenery on the continent.

After leaving Pueblo the railroad runs up the left bank of the Arkansas to Cañon City, and two miles beyond that point enters the Grand Cañon[1]

---

[1] This word, used to describe the huge chasms in the mountains so common throughout this region, is pronounced as though spelt ' can-yon.'

of the Arkansas, for eight miles. At this point the river cuts its way through almost perpendicular walls of granite, which tower up almost straight from the river's edge to a height of nearly 2,000 to 2,500 feet. For the convenience of travellers who wish to study closely this natural wonder, an observation car is here added to the train, from which an unobstructed view of both sides of the cañon is obtained. The gorge winds in and out like some gigantic serpent, and after the first few moments the train seems hopelessly shut in by the frowning walls. In some places the precipice rises so abruptly from the water, that a path for the rails has had to be made by blasting, and in one part of the Royal Gorge, the narrowest and loftiest and most imposing section of the great chasm, the railroad is slung for about 200 feet upon an iron bridge, which hangs from steel girders, spanning the chasm.

The railway system of the United States is a marvel of skill, enterprise and resource. The conditions are entirely different from those in Europe, and great ingenuity has been shown by the engineers in overcoming obstacles such as would at first sight appear fatal to the construction of the iron road. The Colorado Mountains are exceedingly rich in mineral wealth ; and in order that this may be readily transported, the railway has been carried into the very heart of the upper valleys, to such mining centres as Leadville, Ouray, Crested Butte, and Georgetown. The difficulty to be overcome was the rapid rise of the valley, and the impossibility of expending money on tunnels and costly construction. By ingenious improvements in locomotive construction, American engines are built capable of running round curves of less than 300 feet radius, while in England the sharpest turns are rarely less than 1,000 feet radius. The result is that in the United States the rails wind in and out, following the sharp bends of a cañon wall or of a winding valley, tunnelling where that is the only possible method of surmounting the difficulty.

Steep gradients are also overcome by the loop system, or by what is known as the Switchback. One of the most famous examples of the former occurs at Georgetown in Colorado on a branch of the Union Pacific Railroad. The problem was to build a railway from Georgetown to Silver Plume, a mining camp one and a quarter mile up the valley ; but the difference in elevation between the two places is 600 feet. By curving the line in a spiral form and crossing itself by a lofty bridge, the length is extended to four miles, the gradient reduced from 480 feet to 150 feet per mile, and the railroad thus made possible. These Colorado valleys afford considerable evidence in proof of the saying of one of the railroad engineers, 'Where a mule can go I can make a locomotive go.'

Perhaps the most effective example of the switchback system in the Rocky Mountains occurs at the famous Marshall Pass. After leaving the Royal Gorge the railroad continues to climb up the course of the Arkansas river, passing the town of Salida, which lies in a lovely situation on the

The Great Loop at Georgetown.

bosom of a plateau entirely surrounded by lofty mountains. Salida is at an elevation of between 6,000 to 7,000 feet above the sea, and in the course of the next few miles the railroad has to climb up to an elevation of 10,850 feet. The railroad enters the Poncho Gulch, and soon begins to rise in a very marked degree. Two engines are put on the train, which consists of only three or four carriages; as soon as the steep gradient is reached the line begins to wind up the Pass by a series of bold and effective curves. The line is built on the narrow gauge system, to admit of sharper curves. Often, in going round these curves, from the windows of the last car it is possible to look across to the engine running parallel, but of course in the opposite direction. The grades here often reach the limit of ordinary running capacity, being considerably over 200 feet in the mile. Looking up it is possible to see five separate lines of railway one above another which the

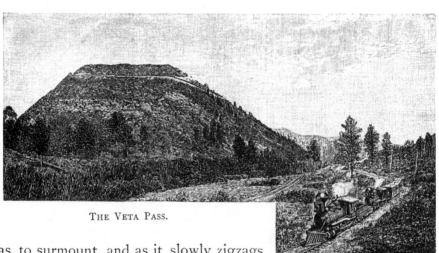

THE VETA PASS.

train has to surmount, and as it slowly zigzags backwards and forwards along these gigantic loops superb views of distant ranges of lofty mountains are obtained. The crest of the Pass is reached across the shoulder of a mountain about 12,000 feet high, the actual summit of the Pass being 10,850 feet above the sea. Anticipations of a still finer view when the actual summit is attained are somewhat rudely dashed when the train comes to a stand in a dark and smoky snow-shed; but while the train waits for a few minutes before starting on the somewhat exciting descent, the passengers are able to make their way out upon a rocky plateau and look down upon the Pacific side of the Pass. There is a satisfaction in feeling that one stands upon the dividing line of the continent; the stream which trickles down from our left hand finds its way ultimately into the Atlantic Ocean, while that which springs a stone's-throw from the right hand, after a tortuous course of over 1,500 miles, finds its way into the great Pacific Ocean.

The western descent is very abrupt and steep, only one engine is necessary, and that travels for the most part with its steam shut off. It is in a journey of this kind that the traveller feels really grateful for the Westinghouse automatic air-brake, by means of which every wheel on the train can be locked in an instant. The only serious risk is any loss of control on the part of the driver, which, if it happened for one half minute, would probably result in the total destruction of the train with all its passengers. Another engineering feat of a similar kind is the construction of the railway up the Veta Pass and over the Duma Mountain.

After leaving the Marshall Pass the main line of railroad runs on through a comparatively tame country to a town called Gunnison. This is the centre for a great mining district, and was designed for a western 'boom;' but the boom has not yet come, and the vast hotel which adjoins the railroad station must be an example of shattered hopes, so far as the proprietors are concerned. A few miles to the west, the road, which now hugs the north bank of the Gunnison River, enters the Black Cañon. Here another observation car is attached to the train. The stream flows through the cañon in a heautiful fresh green current, varying from forty to seventy feet in width, often breaking into rapids. The walls of the cañon are not so lofty as those of the Royal Gorge, but the extent is much greater; they tower above the train, 500, 1,000, and sometimes 1,500 feet, at angles varying from forty-five to sixty degrees, and are often clad with fir and scrub up to the very summit. Sometimes they rise in lofty isolated cones like that named the Currecanti Needle; sometimes they tower aloft like huge castles and are everywhere impressive, and sometimes awe-inspiring. Seen under the brilliant sunshine and blue sky, the place seems hardly to deserve its name; but one can readily believe that if traversed under a cloudy sky or during the night, it would readily respond to its name.

After passing Cimarron, another mountain pass not so formidable as the Marshall Pass has to be surmounted, and then for many hours the train traverses the cañon of the Lower Gunnison; the river has here cut out a winding channel, broad and meandering, but shut in by continuous walls of sandstone. At times the cliff from base to summit is strewn with irregular blocks; at others the surfaces are sharp as if they had been carved with a chisel. The colouring of these great mountain walls is very unusual, the prevailing tone is dust colour—in fact, the whole landscape seems to lie in the grip of the dust demon—but breaking in upon this subdued tone, varying and enriching it, are great veins and columns and cliffs of bright red and terra-cotta sandstone. Sometimes vast masses lie bold and crimson at the top of the cliff, sometimes they cover the face of a wall, while here and there horizontal layers of the sandstone are interspersed with perpendicular blocks of a much lighter colour; in truth, the whole of the scenery for thirty or forty miles would answer in all essential respects to a description of the Nile Valley.

The Grand Cañon of the Colorado.

Soon after leaving Grand Junction the line crosses the Green River, a branch of the Colorado River; and along the course of the latter stream, unfortunately inaccessible to any but the leisured, wealthy, and adventurous traveller, lies the Grand Cañon of the Colorado, by far the most extensive and imposing on the continent. We give an engraving of one of the chief points of interest in this magnificent chasm. This great cañon is a very fine illustration of the geological conditions under which these cañons have come to be, and the reader will probably be glad to have the explanation given in the official record published by the United States Government.[1]

'The Colorado River is formed by the junction of the Grand and the Green Rivers. The Green River is larger than the Grand, and is the upper continuation of the Colorado. Including this river, the whole length of the stream is about two thousand miles. The region of country drained by the Colorado and its tributaries is about eight hundred miles in length, and varies from three hundred to five hundred in width, containing about three hundred thousand square miles. There are two distinct portions of the basin of the Colorado. The lower third is but little above the level of the sea, though here and there ranges of mountains rise to an altitude of from two to six thousand feet. This part of the valley is bounded on the north by a line of cliffs, which present a bold, often vertical step, hundreds or thousands of feet to the table-lands above.

'The upper two-thirds of the basin rises from four to eight thousand feet above the level of the sea. This high region on the east, north, and west, is set with ranges of snow-clad mountains, attaining an altitude above the sea varying from eight to fourteen thousand feet. All winter long, on its mountain-crested rim, snow falls, filling the gorges, half-burying the forests, and covering the crags and peaks with a mantle woven by the winds from the waves of the sea—a mantle of snow. When the summer sun comes, this snow melts and tumbles down the mountain sides in millions of cascades. Ten million cascade brooks unite to form ten thousand torrent creeks; ten thousand torrent creeks unite to form a hundred rivers, beset with cataracts; a hundred rivers unite to form the Colorado, which rolls, a mad, turbid stream, into the Gulf of California.

'Consider the action of one of these streams: its source in the mountains, where the snows fall; its course through the arid plains. Now if at the river's flood storms were falling on the plains, its channel would be cut but little faster than the adjacent country would be washed, and the general level would thus be preserved; but under the conditions here mentioned, the river deepens its bed, as there is much through corrosion, and but little lateral degradation. So all the streams cut deeper and still deeper, until their banks are towering cliffs of solid stone. These deep, narrow gorges are called cañons. For more than a thousand miles along its course, the Colorado

---

[1] *Exploration of the Colorado River of the West in* 1869–1872, by J. W. Powell, pp. 3, 152, and 193.

has cut for itself such a cañon ; but at some few points, where lateral streams join it, the cañon is broken, and narrow transverse valleys divide it properly into a series of cañons.'

Mr. Powell thus explains how these great cañons have come to be what we see them to-day : —

'To a person studying the physical geography of this country, without a knowledge of its geology, it would seem very strange that the river should cut through the mountains, when, apparently, it might have passed around them to the east, through valleys, for there are such along the north side of the Uintas, extending to the east, where the mountains are degraded to hills ; and, passing around these, there are other valleys, extending to the Green, on the south side of the range. Then why did the river run through the mountains ? The first explanation suggested is that it followed a previously formed fissure through the range ; but very little examination will show that this explanation is unsatisfactory. The proof is abundant that the river cut its own channel, that the cañons are gorges of corrosion. Again the question returns to us, why did not the stream turn around this great obstruction, rather than pass through it ? The answer is that the river had the right of way ; in other words, it was running ere the mountains were formed ; not before the rocks of which the mountains are composed were deposited, but before the formations were folded so as to make a mountain range. The contracting or shrivelling of the earth causes the rocks near the surface to wrinkle or fold, and such a fold was started athwart the course of the river. Had it been suddenly formed, it would have been an obstruction sufficient to turn the water in a new course to the east, beyond the extension of the wrinkle ; but the emergence of the fold above the general surface of the country was little or no faster than the progress of the corrosion of the channel. We may say then that the river did not cut its way down through the mountains, from a height of many thousand feet above its present site ; but, having an elevation differing but little, perhaps, from what it now has, as the fold was lifted, it cleared away the obstruction by cutting a cañon, and the walls were thus elevated on either side. The river preserved its level, but the mountains were lifted up ; as the saw revolves on a fixed pivot, while the log through which it cuts is moved along—the river was the saw which cut the mountains in two.'

Here also is Mr. Powell's sketch of the Grand Cañon, which he was the first to thoroughly explore :—

'The varying depths of this cañon, due to the varying altitudes of the plateaus through which it runs, can only be seen from above. As we wind about in the gloomy depths below, the difference between 4,000 and 6,000 feet is not discerned, but the characteristics of the cañon—the scenic features —change abruptly with the change in the altitude of the walls as the faults are passed. In running the channel, which divides the twin plateaus, we pass around the first great southern bend. In the very depths of the cañon we have black granite, with a narrow cleft through which a great river plunges. This granite portion of the walls is carved with deep gulches and embossed with pinnacles and towers. Above are broken, ragged, nonconformable rocks, in many places sloping back at a low angle. Clambering over these, we reach rocks lying in horizontal beds; some are soft, many very hard; the softer strata are washed out, the harder remain as shelves. Everywhere there are side gulches and cañons, so that these gulches are set about ten thousand dark, gloomy alcoves. One might imagine that this was intended for the library of the gods; and it was. The shelves are not for books, but form the stony leaves of one great book. He who would read the language of the universe may dig out letters here and there, and with them spell the words, and read in a slow and imperfect way, but still so as to understand a little the story of creation.'

During that part of its course which forms the Marble and the Grand Cañons, the river runs across the north-western corner of Arizona. It then turns to the south, and during the last stage of its career forms the western boundary of that State, finally emptying into the Gulf of California. Arizona is almost unknown as yet to the tourist, and is very sparsely peopled, even for the district west of the Rocky Mountains. But it has some very fine scenery, and bids fair, on

GIANT CACTUS, ARIZONA.

account of the warm and dry winter climate, to become a favourite resort for invalids. The Southern Pacific Railway now traverses the State. The heat in summer is very great, and the vegetation is sub-tropical—palms, aloes, and various species of cactus which here reach a very considerable size.

To the east of Arizona lies the State of New Mexico, and in the north-western portion of that State is the home of the Zuñi Indians, famous for the great pueblos, or combined houses in which they reside. 'Imagine,' says one of the few men who have been able to study these pueblos at his leisure, 'numberless long box-shaped, adobe ranches connected with one another in extended rows and squares, with others less and less numerous piled up on them lengthwise and crosswise, in two, three, even six storeys, each receding from the one below it like the steps of a broken stairflight, and you can gain a fair conception of the architecture of Zuñi. Every-where this structure bristles with ladder-poles, chimneys, and rafters. The ladders are heavy and long, and lean at all angles against the roof. The Indians assemble for their numerous dances upon the topmost terraces of this strange city.' The engraving represents the Knife Dance, one of the most savage of these. 'The dancers file in through the covered way, preceded by a priest, and arrange themselves in a line across the court. Their costumes and masks are smeared with blood, and their beards and hair long and streaming. In their right hand the performers carry huge, leaf-shaped, blood-stained knives of stone which, during the movements of the dance, they brandish wildly in the air in time and accompaniment to their wild song and regular steps.' This dance is performed when any sacrifice of life, either human or animal, is to be made. It was the ancient war-dance of the tribe.

The eastern boundary of the Territory of Utah is crossed soon after leaving Grand Junction, but Salt Lake City still lies a long journey to the west. But at the towns of Provo and Bingham are many evidences of the agricultural skill and farming industry of the Mormons. When, on July 24, 1847, Brigham Young with his 142 hardy pioneers entered the valley at the eastern end, after the long and toilsome journey over the great central plain and through the almost impassable mountains, there was reason on his side when he thought that at length they had found a home in which they could never be disturbed.

The Mormon community, or as they call themselves, the Church of Jesus Christ of Latter Day Saints, had already passed through very trying experiences. Joseph Smith, the founder, was born at Sharon in Vermont, December 23, 1805; and in 1820, when living with his parents at Man-chester in New York State, he began to have his visions. He alleged that on the night of September 23, 1823, the angel Moroni appeared to him and revealed that the Bible of the Western Continent, a supplement to the

New Testament, was buried near Manchester. In 1827 he went to this place, and there the angel gave him a stone box containing a book six inches thick, made of thin gold plates eight inches by seven, covered with writing in 'reformed Egyptian.' The book was fortunately accompanied by a pair of wonderful spectacles called 'Urim and Thummim,' and by their

THE KNIFE DANCE.

aid the mysterious characters could be read. Smith's education having been defective, he employed a certain Oliver Cowdery as amanuensis, whilst he himself from behind a curtain dictated the translation. A farmer named Martin Harris found the necessary money, and in 1830 the Book of Mormon was published. It was prefaced by a sworn statement, signed by Oliver Cowdery, David Whitmer, and Martin Harris, in which they affirm that

' we declare with words of soberness, that an angel of God came down from heaven, and he brought and laid before our eyes, that we beheld and saw the plates and the engravings thereon ; and we know that it is by the grace of God the Father, and our Lord Jesus Christ, that we beheld and bear record that these things are true,'—and more to the same effect. This book, and the fact that the plates mysteriously disappeared, enabled Smith to impose upon the credulous. In it he was declared to be a 'prophet' who ought to be obeyed.

The above is the account Smith professed to give of the book, but according to the modern critical spirit the whole story was a romance written by a man named Spalding in 1812. It was copied by a man named Rigdon, who gave it to Smith, the latter making use of it for his own purposes. A few years later the three men who had signed the declaration renounced Mormonism and declared it false ; but in a copy of the Book of Mormon which the author purchased at Salt Lake City in 1890, it is still printed as though it were true.

Smith's preaching and his book at once began to attract attention and to win believers. In 1830 a conference was held at Fayette, New York State, and in the same year Smith obtained a useful 'revelation,' proclaiming him to be 'seer, translator, prophet, apostle of Jesus Christ, and elder of the church.' He now began to baptise and formally enrol followers. His character did not stand high in his own neighbourhood, and so he removed to Kirtland, Ohio, with thirty adherents. Here, also by revelation, he started a bank which issued worthless notes, and this led to Smith and Rigdon being tarred and feathered.

In 1833 the 'church' was organised under three presidents—Smith, Rigdon, and F. G. Williams. The movement would probably have come to an end in this early stage, had it not been for the advent in Kirtland in 1832 of Brigham Young, then thirty years old. Possessed of very great gifts, executive ability, business capacity, effective speech, Young thus early became the real support of the movement which had been nearly, but unfortunately not quite, ruined by Smith's sensuality. In 1835 twelve 'apostles' were chosen, and it was resolved to send these out to convert the 'Gentiles.' In 1836 a temple was built at Kirtland. Young went through the Eastern States ; Orson Hyde and H. C. Kimball came to England, and all three made many converts.

In 1838 the Kirtland bank failed, and Smith and Rigdon fled to Missouri. Dissensions, due largely to Smith's evil character, broke out, and the opposing sections took up arms. The State authorities arrested Smith and Rigdon, charging them with treason, murder, and felony, and drove their adherents, 15,000 in number, into Illinois, where they settled near a place called Commerce. Smith escaped, obtained a charter and founded a city called Nauvoo. Smith's profligacy led to the notorious 'revelation' as

SALT LAKE CITY.

to polygamy. In 1844 he was arrested and imprisoned; but on June 27 a mob seized him and his brother Hyram and shot them both. This savage act did much to efface the impression of Smith's worse than indifferent character, gave him the appearance of a martyr, and resulted in an extraordinary impulse to the Mormon movement.

Brigham Young succeeded Smith, and as the legislature of Illinois repealed the charter they had previously granted to Nauvoo, he determined to emigrate the whole community to the Far West. Utah was selected, and in 1847 the foundations of the Mormon State were laid in the Salt Lake Valley—free for ever, as Brigham Young fondly hoped, from any further interference on the part of State authorities. A flood tide of immigration set in, and in 1849 the community was organised under the name of Deseret, a term said to mean 'the land of the honey-bee,' a legislature was appointed, and a constitution approved and sent to Washington. This Congress refused to ratify, and in 1850, as a compromise, Utah was organised as a Territory. A long and intermittent struggle thus began between Brigham Young and the United States Government, which lasted on and off for the rest of his life. In 1871 Young was arrested for polygamy and declared criminal; but this action had little result. Young died in 1877, leaving seventeen wives, fifty-six children, and a fortune of £400,000. In the same year John D. Lee, one of the leading men, was executed for his share in an emigrant massacre in 1857. The Government has compelled every Mormon with more than one wife to put away forever all wives but the one first married, he at the same time making all due provision for their temporal necessities. For political reasons the proper church officials will probably soon confirm this action, and make it binding upon all Mormons; the public opinion of the Mormon community, especially of the younger portion, having long been in favour of this enactment.

Differences of opinion may and will exist as to the theology, ecclesiastical polity and social ethics of the Mormons. But there can hardly be a difference of opinion as to their skill in husbandry, their business enterprise, and commercial integrity. They have turned the barren and arid valley into a fertile and flourishing land. By irrigation, by constant care and attention, they have caused the wilderness to blossom as the rose. Salt Lake City, in its size and life and prosperity, is a good testimonial to Mormon thrift and energy. This famous metropolis is well situated in a plain 4,300 feet above the sea, encircled by an amphitheatre of mountains. It has a fine and equable climate. It is regularly laid out, possesses some handsome and many large buildings, with hotels, electric tramways, telegraph, telephone, and the manifold other conveniences of a large American city.

The chief edifices in Salt Lake City are connected with the Mormon religion. Most of them are contained in what is known as the Temple Block, ten acres in extent, surrounded by a high wall. At the head of them stands the Large Tabernacle, designed—like so much else in Salt Lake City—by the active brain of Brigham Young. It was to be substantial and convenient for large assemblies. These requirements are fully met. Begun in July 1864, it was finished and dedicated in October 1867. The exterior is as unattractive as any building could be, presenting the appearance of a gigantic dish-cover. Viewed from the interior it is more pleasing. It has very large seating accommodation, and it is certainly possessed of fine acoustic properties. The shape is an oval, 250 feet long, 150 feet wide, and 70 feet high, the roof having no central support. The circuit of the

AN ELECTRIC TRAMWAY WORKED BY OVERHEAD CONNECTION.

gallery is 480 feet, and it is 30 feet wide. The number of seats is sometimes given as high as 12,000, and it certainly can accommodate 9,000 in comfort. There are twenty doors, and the huge structure can be emptied with the greatest ease in three or four minutes. An enormous organ, the desks of the officials who preside at the service, seats for singers in the choir, and the platforms for addresses occupy the western end.

In another part of the Temple enclosure stands the Assembly Hall, built of granite at a cost of £18,000. This is smaller, very well decorated, and capable of seating from 2,000 to 3,000 people. This structure was finished in 1880.

But by far the most costly of these great buildings is the still (1891) unfinished Salt Lake Temple. From east to west this measures 186½ feet, and the width is 99 feet. There are fine towers at each corner, and a centre tower at both the east and west ends. The east centre tower is to be 200 feet high. The substance used is finely cut and finished granite brought from the Wasatch Mountains, twenty miles away. The site was consecrated in February 1853, and the foundation stone laid in April of the same year. It is said that the uncertain relations with the United States Government have delayed the construction; also that it affords a convenient plea for levying tithes and free-will offerings. Over £1,000,000, derived entirely from the tithes levied upon the members of the Mormon Church, have already been expended upon it.

Most visitors to Salt Lake City arrive, in all probability, with pre-possessions and prejudices regarding the peculiar views of the great majority of the people. For their Biblical and social tenets it is hard to have any respect, except that always bestowed upon men holding religious views conscientiously, however absurd and mistaken they may appear. When the author visited the city he was fortunate in having considerable opportunity of studying the people in their public assemblies. He attended several meetings in the great tabernacle. One was a concert for the benefit of the schools of the city, at which about 3,000 persons were present, the vast majority being members of the Mormon Church. A better-dressed, better-behaved, and on the whole a more intelligent audience would not be seen at similar gatherings in New York, Boston, or London. Another occasion was the annual gathering of the Young Men's Mutual Improvement Societies of Utah, held on a Sunday morning. At this sacred pieces were sung, prayers offered, speeches by young delegates were delivered, and then came the only thing which differed greatly from what would occur at a similar meeting elsewhere in America or in England. An elaborate oration was delivered upon 'The Life of Joseph the Prophet.'

The orator was a man evidently well-versed in the art of public speech, and he gave a clear and interesting sketch of the life and influence of Joseph Smith from the Mormon point of view. It need scarcely be said that this differs widely from the current Gentile version. According to the orator Smith was a prophet, and his revelations were of equal importance to those of Jesus Christ, and in fact were absolutely necessary, in order to supplement and complete that recorded in the New Testament. He then described the scenes at Nauvoo, which resulted in the death of Joseph Smith, and drew a vivid and powerful picture of the Mormon prophet dying as a martyr for the new truth which he had been inspired by God to reveal to the nineteenth century. The close of the address was an impassioned appeal to the young men of Utah to walk worthily of their great exemplar, and to be willing in these days of persecution to suffer death on behalf of the truth revealed by him to the Latter Day Saints.

It was certainly a strange experience to sit in a public building in the enlightened republic of the United States, a unit in a great audience, and quietly listen to a capable speaker as he described the career of the Mormon prophet in terms suitable in the ears of a Christian man only for the Head of the Christian Church Himself!

The ordinary service in the Mormon Tabernacle is held only on the Sunday afternoon at two o'clock. On the occasion just referred to the service consisted of singing, of impassioned prayers for an outpouring of the Holy Spirit, interspersed with addresses. A long harangue was delivered by one of the apostles, remarkable chiefly for the fanatical belief in Mormonism, the extravagant eulogy of the 'Prophet Joseph,' and the confident assertion of the power of the Church of the Latter Day Saints to win the final victory over all other forms of belief which it displayed. There was also a short speech by Wilford Woodruff, the successor to Joseph Smith, Brigham Young, and John Taylor in the headship of the church, and one of the few survivors who took any active part in the stormy scenes at Nauvoo in 1846. The impression he produced was that of a fairly capable, but in no sense remarkable man, who had reached his present eminence more by reason of his association with the abler leaders of the past than any unusual intellectual gifts or qualities which he possessed. He let fall some oracular utterances to the effect that he also had some revelations to make to the church, had that been the proper time to do so.

Between the first and the third 'Sentiments,' as some of the addresses were called, a kind of equivalent for the Christian Breaking of Bread took place. About twenty very large baskets of electro-ware, containing large slices of bread, and about as many large tankards, together with some forty silver cups, had been placed upon a long table ranged across the western end of the hall; early in the service twenty men ranged themselves on either side of the table and proceeded to break the bread rapidly into small pieces. They waited until a pause occurred in the programme, and then one of them offered a short prayer. The programme immediately resumed, and forthwith the twenty men proceeded to distribute the bread to every one in the audience. When the bread had been thus given to all, another prayer was offered at the table, and then they carried the tankards and cups through the congregation to distribute the water in like fashion.

The enormous size of the ordinary congregation at the Tabernacle is due to the fact that the Church of Latter Day Saints in Salt Lake City, have only this one place of worship, and hence all who are present at worship must come to that one meeting. Babies abounded in the great audience, children were allowed to roam about with a freedom unknown in any ordinary Christian service, women were very numerous, but the proportion of men present was very much larger than is at all customary in Christian churches. Scanning as carefully as one could the 6,000 present, the impression was received—perhaps only to be expected—that the average of intelligence and refinement was much lower than in the smaller assembly present at the concert.

There is a good deal to amuse and instruct the stranger in the wide busy streets of the Mormon capital. One of the oldest buildings in the city is the *Deseret News* office, the official organ of the Mormon Church, which began its issue in 1850. Behind this building are the warehouses and yards connected with the General Tithing Storehouse. From the beginning, Mormon law has been very rigid in exacting from every Latter Day Saint a tenth of his income for ecclesiastical purposes. And as his income increases—and in Salt Lake City very few indeed have remained stationary—so has the amount of his contribution. But it is all paid in kind. The farmer pays the products of his farm, the stockman the increase of his herds, the artisan and the labourer pay in manual toil. Hence at the Tithing Store an extraordinary supply of commodities of many kinds accumulates, and these in turn are paid out to the men who work on the temples, to clerks and public officials, to the poor, and to friendly Indians ; and they are also largely bartered for other needed merchandise.

A short distance beyond this pile of buildings stand a group of houses inhabited by Brigham Young, known respectively as the Lion House and the Beehive House. On the opposite of the street is the great mansion known as the Gardo House, said to have been built by Brigham Young for his favourite wife, but never permanently occupied by him.

The railroad to Ogden skirts for many miles the Great Salt Lake. This inland sea stands 4,200 feet above the level of the ocean, and is seventy-five miles long with an average breadth of thirty. Several streams empty into it, but it has no known outlet. It is very shallow, the water clear but intensely salt, and so buoyant that it is next to impossible to sink in it. A bath in it is said to be very refreshing, although the body needs to be washed after it in fresh water. It has become a favourite watering place for the inhabitants of Salt Lake City ; Lake Park, a tastefully laid out pleasure resort, being the headquarters for this kind of amusement.

Near the north-eastern corner of the Salt Lake is the town of Ogden, where the Denver and Rio Grande railways connect with the Central Pacific. It was near this town, at a place called Promontory Point, that the railroad from San Francisco met the railroad from the East on May 10, 1869. The last tie was made of California laurel adorned with silver, and the last four spikes were solid silver and gold. Whether these are still *in situ* we did not learn. From this point westward to the Sierra Nevada Mountains extends the district that in the old maps is called the Great American Desert. The surface soil is alkaline earth, arid and dusty, and clad only with the scattered tufts of sage grass. The slightest breeze or the passage of a herd of cattle raises suffocating clouds of fine alkali dust, which penetrates into every nook and cranny of the passing train. And yet, unpromising as this region appears, it is becoming more and more evident that skilful irrigation can and does turn it into a fruitful garden. Hence, wherever the level of the land, in combination with advancing civilization, permits of it, irrigation works are carefully carried out.

At the various wayside stations the Red Indian is very much to the fore, idling about the stations, and is remarkable, both in the person of the braves, and even more of the squaws, for excessive ugliness. The journey across the Sierra Nevada range is a repetition on a somewhat smaller scale of the great Rocky Mountains plateaux and peaks and passes, and from Oakland a pleasant sail across the wide harbour brings the traveller to San Francisco and the Pacific shore.

THE BIG LOOP ON THE SHASTA RAILWAY, NEAR McCLOUD.
(From a photograph by Taber, of San Francisco.)

From a photograph]

THE YOSEMITE VALLEY FROM ARTIST POINT.

[*By Taber, of San Francisco.*

From Harper's Magazine.

SAN FRANCISCO BAY AND ALCATRAZ ISLAND.

CHAPTER VIII.

THE PACIFIC COAST AND THE YOSEMITE VALLEY.

HATEVER route the traveller follows to the Pacific slope, be it the Northern, Central, or Southern Pacific Railway, he is certain sooner or later to find himself in San Francisco, the metropolis of California; although, as elsewhere, the relatively unimportant town of Sacramento is the State capital. The city occupies the northern end of a peninsula washed by the Pacific Ocean on the west, and by the waters of San Francisco Bay on the east. The original site presented a most unpromising appearance; it was occupied by a cluster of low sterile hills, separated by valleys filled with rock and sand dunes. The final selection of the place as a settlement was due to the splendid harbour afforded by the bay, the only really good one on the Pacific coast for hundreds of miles. Although there are traditions of earlier visits, the actual discovery seems to have been made by Spanish monks in 1769. In 1776 a permanent lodgment, consisting of a presidio or fortified settlement, and a mission was made, and named San

N

Francisco de los Dolores. In 1830 it had a population of about 200, composed of Spanish soldiers and adherents of the mission.

California was annexed by the United States in the year 1846. Immigration at once commenced, and in less than two years the population had increased to over 1,000. In January 1848, at a place called Coloma, about sixty miles east of Sacramento City, the world-famous discovery of gold was made. The secret could not be kept, and the news rapidly spread. A contemporary narrative gives us the following picture: 'Soon the neighbourhood swarmed with diggers, and within a few days after the first discovery upwards of 1,200 people were busily at work with spades, shovels, knives, wooden bowls, and all manner of implements, excavating, riddling, and washing earth for the precious particles it contained. Over all California the excitement was prodigious. The few ships that could get away, and travellers and expresses by land, spread the news far and wide over remote seas and through foreign climes. The circles of excitement grew wider and wider, and scarcely lost strength as they spread.'

The natural and inevitable result of this was to increase the population by leaps and bounds, and by December 1850 it had reached 25,000. From that time to the present the growth has been steady, the census of 1890 giving a population of 306,000. The original buildings were almost entirely of wood, the materials in many cases having been brought from the Atlantic States, and like all large western towns the city has suffered from fires. In the year 1850 no less than three great conflagrations took place, destroying property to the value of £1,500,000. The result of this was to fix the public attention upon fire-proof buildings, and led to the early use of granite, iron, and brick.

The chief business quarter of San Francisco lies to the north-east of the peninsula, and is well and regularly laid out. The great business thoroughfare is Market Street, a very wide roadway lined with handsome business premises, and traversed by several parallel lines of tramways which run from the ferry and the harbours some three miles inland. Many of the handsomest private residences of the city are on California Street Hill. Cable car lines traverse the city in many different directions, and climb hills which are sufficiently steep to make the stranger a trifle nervous. The city possesses many fine buildings, among which may be mentioned the City Hall, not yet finished although twenty-five years have elapsed since it was commenced, the United States Mint, the Merchants' Exchange, and the Bank of California. San Francisco claims to have the largest hotels in the United States, and as far as appearance goes this claim seems to be well founded. The Palace Hotel in Market Street is a gigantic pile, nine storeys high, 350 feet long, and 275 feet wide, and is said to have cost nearly £700,000.

The features of San Francisco most likely to arrest the attention of the visitor are the Harbour, China Town, and the Golden Gate. As already noted

CALIFORNIA STREET, SAN FRANCISCO.

the harbour is the finest on the Pacific coast. It is a large bay, extending north and south, entered from the Pacific Ocean by a strait five miles long and about one mile in width. The length of the bay is forty miles, and its width, just opposite the city, seven miles. The northern shores around the part known as San Pablo Bay are mountainous and well-wooded, and

A STREET IN CHINA TOWN, SAN FRANCISCO.

the great expanse of water dotted with lovely islets, and bounded by the near and distant mountain outlines, afford an almost exhaustless series of lovely and delightful views. The bay is crossed in many directions by large and well-equipped steam ferry-boats, which enable the passengers to enjoy to the full the manifold beauties of the scene.

China Town is an extraordinary phenomenon. Within the limits of Sacramento, Jackson, Dupont and Pacific Streets about 40,000 Chinamen

A Chinese Actor in the Theatre of San Francisco.

have transformed the district into a Chinese city. The buildings, it is true, present a western aspect, but the vast majority of the faces of men, women, and children belong to the Mongol type. The signs above the shops are all in Chinese, and the buildings have been adapted, so far as possible, to Chinese use. It is the fashion for strangers to be taken through this district by men who profess to be duly qualified guides; but, unless time presses very severely, much the best way is to stroll quietly through the quarter. Of course, if such places as the numerous gambling houses and opium dens are visited, it will be wiser to go accompanied by a policeman. The opium dens are generally dark and dismal places lit only by the lamps used to light the opium pipes, and around the walls are rough wooden pallets upon which the victims of this fatal habit lie in the various stages of opium influence. There are several Joss houses or temples, and there are many Chinese restaurants.

One of the most popular sights presented by this novel heathen settlement is the Chinese theatre. Chinamen are passionately fond of gambling and of dramatic representations. One of the two theatres in this quarter is capable of containing about one thousand spectators, and is packed night after night from floor to ceiling. The drama represented is continued from night to night, and often takes a fortnight or so for its complete presentation.

After a study of China Town one appreciates more intelligently the position taken by many Americans with regard to the Chinese. This is, that whereas Irishmen, Germans, Italians and others soon become citizens, and thus form an integral part of the Republic, the Chinaman never does: he comes simply to make money; he stays only so long as it suits his purpose; he continues an alien; if he dies he makes arrangements for his body to be returned to his native land; while the peculiarity of his habits, and the smallness of the sum upon which he can live, render him a formidable competitor in the labour market. China Town is conclusive proof of the power of the 'Heathen Chinee' to transform the very heart of a Californian· city according to his own habits and desires, and to remain there unaffected to any appreciable extent by Western civilisation. Nevertheless, after giving full weight to these views, it still remains an open question whether the policy of attempting to exclude the Chinese from the country has been either wise or just.

The Golden Gate is the narrow entrance which admits the in-coming vessel from the Pacific into the harbour. It is formed by two bold head-lands jutting out into the ocean, and upon the southernmost, known as Port Lobos, are two very popular places of resort—the Cliff House, a kind of hotel; and the Sutro Heights, a fine private residence with splendid gardens, through which the public are allowed to pass. The Golden Gate is reached by a drive of six miles; but the more popular route is the cable cars, and the continuance of the journey on steam cars. This trip affords ample evidence of the bleak and desolate appearance which the site must have presented originally, since even now many bare and barren stretches of rock and of sand are to be seen. From the Cliff House the eye ranges

THE LARGEST TELESCOPE IN THE WORLD.

over the vast Pacific Ocean, the low sandy beach of which stretches far away to the south. Close by the hotel is the noted seal rock, and from the piazza a large number of sea lions may be seen wriggling over the rock or basking in the sun, while the peculiar barking noise which they make can be heard in the intervals of the thunderous roar of the Pacific surge.

The suburbs of San Francisco abound in beautiful places like San Raphael; but the most noted from a scientific standpoint is the Lick Observatory, remarkable, not only for the perfection of its equipment, but still more because it now possesses the largest telescope in the world. Mr. Lick died at San Francisco in 1876, leaving a large fortune for the purpose of building this telescope. It is 60 feet in focal length, and has an object glass 36 inches in diameter; the site chosen for the observatory is the summit of Mount Hamilton, 4,000 feet above the level of the sea, about sixty miles from San Francisco, and about twenty miles by road from San

From a photograph]   A PALM GROVE IN SOUTHERN CALIFORNIA.   [*by Taber, of San Francisco.*

José, the nearest town. Our engraving represents the great telescope as in constant use in the dome of the observatory. The institution is the property of the University of California.

Southern California has become notable in recent years for the abundance and excellence of its watering-places, and hence is yearly growing in favour as a health resort. Chief among these are Santa Barbara, Los Angeles, the largest city in South California, and San Diego. All of these towns are splendidly supplied with large and convenient hotels, whilst the rich sub-tropical vegetation is a constant pleasure to the inhabitants. The whole district is fast becoming the chief fruit garden of the United States; orange groves and vineyards abound, and the great San Joaquin Valley is one of the most fertile districts on the continent. The improvement of railway communication of recent years has greatly developed the trade in fruit and wine. Gold mining is still one of the chief industries of the State, and for this purpose, and also for irrigation, water engineering has there reached a high level. By means of flumes, as they are termed, water is conveyed many miles for the various operations connected with agriculture and mining.

San Francisco is also the chief starting-point for a trip to that wonderful mountain district known as the Yosemite Valley. The great Sierra Nevada, or Snowy Range of mountains traverses the western part of the continent parallel to the Pacific, and from fifty to one hundred miles distant from the ocean. The width of this great mountain chain is from seventy-five to one hundred miles, and it runs across the entire State of California. The eastern slopes are very gentle, but on the western side the range is furrowed by deep and precipitous cañons. The most remarkable scenery within the limits of California centres in three notable districts : the numerous domes and granite pinnacles which overhang Owens Lake on the south ; the glorious solitary snow-crowned peaks of Mount Shasta on the north ; and the Yosemite Valley midway between.

A FLUME IN CALIFORNIA.

The upper part of the vast mountain range consists of a series of stupendous granite table-lands, from which spring the giant peaks of Mount Whitney, Mount Lyell, and many others. The Yosemite Valley presents the appearance of a gigantic break or fault in the granite backbone of the chain. If the reader can imagine cliffs varying from 3,000 to 5,000 feet in height to have slowly receded from one another until they stand from half to three-quarters of a mile apart, with a nearly level valley floor between, through which a mountain stream slowly winds for a distance of about six miles, he will gain a fair general idea of the valley. It is situated about 140 miles to the south-east of San Francisco, but the route usually followed —viz., by railroad to Raymond, and thence by coach—is over 250 miles. The long and arduous stage journey is broken by a night's rest at the Wawona Hotel, which is also the starting-point for the visit to the Mariposa Grove of Big Trees.

The stages are not very comfortable, and the road traverses such mountainous country that they are swung on very solid leather springs, which have but a feeble influence in lessening the shock of the manifold bumps and jolts; but the difficulties and fatigue of the journey are lightened by the many varieties of hill and valley and forest through which the road passes, and by the superb and extraordinary profusion and variety of lovely wild flowers to be seen on every hand. These present in the proper season a constant succession of exquisite blooms, the whole expanse of land on either side of the road being at times covered with them: azaleas, Mariposa lilies, and many other unfamiliar flowers, yellow, scarlet, pink, blue and violet, sometimes singly, but often in masses. This ride, in the months of May or June, amply justifies the world-wide reputation possessed by the wild flowers of California.

Starting early the next morning, from the Wawona Hotel, a ride of six or seven hours brings us to the far-famed valley. The difficulty of the approach can be understood from the fact that by whichever route the traveller comes he must climb 3,000 or 3,500 feet higher than the level of the valley before he can obtain an entrance into it. After leaving the valley the Merced River runs through a cañon too precipitous and crooked to admit of any road running through it, and hence from whatever direction the approach be made one of the walls of the valley has to be surmounted, and the level of the valley reached by a road which winds down the mountain side. This method has one great advantage, viz., it gives as the first view of the valley the survey of its entire length shown in the engraving on page 176. After passing Inspiration Point, as the spot is called whence the most extensive general view is obtained, the road plunges in long curves rapidly down 3,000 feet of mountain, affording many different views of the great chasm in the granite rocks. Only on reaching the level of the Merced River can the gigantic proportions of the magnificent gateway which Nature has provided to one of her greatest marvels be fully appreciated. On the left hand there rises, grim and stately, the enormous mass of granite, fitly named El Capitan, which thrusts its great square shoulder sharply forward into the valley, presenting a nearly perpendicular cliff of cold, grey granite 3,300 feet in height—a fit guard for such a treasure. On the right hand stands a lower cliff, and over a deep depression in the centre of this leaps the lovely Bridal Veil Fall, which descends in its first bound a distance of 630 feet, and then rushes down the remaining 300 feet in a series of lovely cascades.

After passing this superb natural porch, the imposing features of the valley come into sight one by one, and as the road winds in and out the traveller is able to see them from many different points of view, each in succession possessing some special charm or grandeur, and appearing to surpass those which have gone before. Even the fatigue and discomfort and dust of the long stage ride from Wawona have but little influence in diminishing the pleasure and excitement of this first experience. Immediately beyond the Bridal Veil Fall rises the massive pile, 2,600 feet high, and so steep as to be nearly bare of vegetation, of the Cathedral Rock. Attached to this, and seen first in profile, are two columnar masses of granite, each over 500 feet high, called the Cathedral Spires. From a point a little further up the valley, these are seen with the huge Cathedral Rock directly behind them, and then they

ENTERING THE YOSEMITE VALLEY.

resemble very closely the two western towers of some gigantic Gothic cathedral. As if to preserve the balance, on the other side of the valley, only a mile away, three great peaks rise symmetrically one above another, and are known as the Three Brothers ; and before the eye can well take in their beautiful proportions it is fascinated by another mass on the right hand side, which rises up like some Titanic watch-tower, and which, evidently from this resemblance, has been named Sentinel Rock. Nothing could be finer than this enormous rocky peak as it rises up into the clear sky,

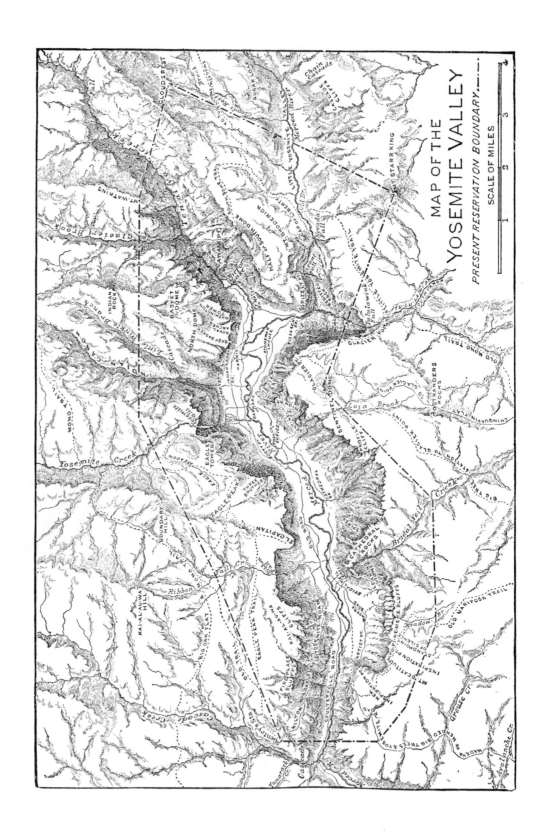

MAP OF THE
YOSEMITE VALLEY

PRESENT RESERVATION BOUNDARY.___

SCALE OF MILES

1,000 feet above the neighbouring cliff, mounting guard age after age. Immediately opposite Sentinel Rock is the Yosemite Fall, which is in some respects the most remarkable in the valley, especially if seen at a time when the water is full. The vertical height of the fall is 2,600 feet taken in three sections; first, a perpendicular fall of 1,500 feet, then a series of cascades for about 600 feet, and a final plunge of 400 feet. On a quiet evening in the early summer this fall dominates the valley; fascinating the eye with its wonderful beauty, and filling the ear with the distant thunder of its many waters.

About two miles beyond the Yosemite Falls, the main valley comes to an abrupt termination, but three smaller branches or cañons penetrate further into the heart of the Sierras. Through the central valley flows the Merced River, fed by the perennial snows of Mount Lyell, and descending from the upper ranges of the cliffs in two magnificent falls, and a series of grand cascades. Through the left hand or northern valley flows the Tenaiya fork of the Merced River, commemorating in its name the old chief of the Yosemite Indians, who was ruling the tribe when the valley was first visited by white men in 1851. Through

SENTINEL ROCK.

the southern flows the Illilouette. These cañons break up the inner end of the valley into a series of grand cliffs.

At the base of the vast cliff known as Half Dome, appropriately closing that end of the valley by an inaccessible precipice rising to a height of 4,700 feet, is the chief hotel—the Stoneman House. For some years past the Yosemite has been a national park under the direct control of the State authorities of California. Under their auspices the roads leading into the valley have been greatly improved, and they have also provided this large and comfortable hotel. Living in such a spot can hardly be other than expensive, since all the provisions have to be carried very long distances by road. Consequently the tariff is high, but not unreasonably so, and the management has a tendency to become autocratic. It is here that the daily stages start and stop, and here also horses and guides may be obtained for the very numerous magnificent mountain excursions which the district affords. No hotel could be more splendidly situated. On every side it is surrounded by objects calculated to impress the imagination and

From a photograph]   THE STONEMAN HOUSE.   *[by Taber, of San Francisco.*

to kindle enthusiasm. It is seated near the confluence of the streams which unite to swell the Merced River. On the one hand, the North Dome rises nearly perpendicularly to a height of 3,500 feet; and on the other, Glacier Point, over 3,000 feet high, seems to almost overhang the building. Directly behind it towers up the Half Dome, for long years considered absolutely inaccessible, and from its curious shape, exactly described by the name, arresting the attention at every turn. The hotel is also encircled by a bewildering profusion of lesser precipices, peaks, cañons and waterfalls, any one of which in other neighbourhoods would be considered well worth a long journey to see.

Of the splendid mountain excursions, large and small, which may be made, there is no limit save those imposed by the time and energy at the disposal of the sojourner. One of the pleasant features of life at the Stoneman House, is the daily bustle, morning and evening, caused by the departure and return of the mountaineering parties. To those who are lounging at their ease on the wide cool and shady piazza, too lazy or too feeble to ascend the trails, the arrival of the daily stages with their loads of nearly dust-smothered humanity, is a source of constant interest and amusement.

Few visitors give the time needed for visits to more than a few of the most accessible summits. If one such trip must suffice, undoubtedly the choice should fall upon Glacier Point. From the hotel verandah he can see, more than half a mile above his head in the sky the goal he seeks; but to reach that point a long and a somewhat rough journey has to be accomplished. Walking is at a discount everywhere in the United States, and nowhere is it treated with more disdain than in the Yosemite. The only correct way according to local ideas, therefore, of visiting any of the numerous notable peaks is on the back of a horse or mule. This method is not quite so luxurious as it seems, since the Merced River not unfrequently floods all the ordinary roads of the valley to a depth of two or three feet, and the trails are often anything but easy walking. The ascent of the cliffs begins two miles down the valley, and follows a trail or mountain path which during the first stage winds up the tremendous rocky face presented to the valley by Sentinel Rock. Standing on the level of the valley, and looking up at this massive wall, it seems hardly possible for even an expert climber to find a safe foothold, to say nothing of a horse or mule. One of the great peculiarities of the Yosemite cliffs, due in some degree to the fact that they are granite, is the very small amount of fragments and débris lying at their base. In the lapse of ages a certain amount has fallen, and the wall faces, which from a distance seem smooth and unbroken, do present here and there convenient ledges. Otherwise the cliff could only be scaled by the aid of wings.

The moment the trail is struck it begins to rise rapidly, and at the end of the first few minutes a series of glorious views begin to lighten the fatigue of the way. The trail clings to the surface of the cliff, and rises by a series of steep and abrupt zigzags. At one turn of the zigzag the Yosemite Fall on the opposite side of the valley is in full view; at the other turn the trail seems to have a very precarious attachment to the face of Sentinel Rock, towering aloft 1,000 or 1,500 feet above it. These alternate views of fall and cliff are repeated at each turn in the ascent, the successive changes in elevation only discovering fresh beauties in the scene. The great volume of water pouring over the Yosemite Falls fascinates the eye with its snowy whiteness sharply outlined against the sombre cliff, and as the path rises to the level of the base of the first great fall, the thunder of the water seems to fill the whole valley. At parts of the journey the ascent is so steep and the turns so sharp that as many as five or six sections of the trail rise one above another all in view at the same time. The enjoyment of the rider is occasionally marred by the objection-

A YOSEMITE TRAIL.

able habit which all the Yosemite beasts have of enjoying the prospect—which at times is very extensive—from the extreme edge of the outer bend of the trail. There they will stop, and peer down, as if to estimate the distance already tra-versed, and at such moments the rider's eye looking straight over his horse's nose falls on the valley floor some 2,000 feet beneath, and with no intervening object in view to lessen the impression of eleva-tion and of insecurity. At such moments he is glad to recall the guide's assurances that he could not push one of these beasts from the path even if he tried.

About half-way up the ascent, Union Point is reached, affording a grand view of the entrance of the valley. Here a short rest is taken, and the remainder of the climb is not so steep. The path winds over a great shoulder of the moun-tain, and—unless it is late in the season —over snow drifts, and through some pine woods to the summit. This is not an isolated cone or peak, but a mountain plateau which juts out into the air; and from its extreme angle —Glacier Point proper—most superb views are enjoyed. These are of various kinds. It is possible, as represented in the engraving, to stand on the edge of the rock and look down the sheer 3,000 feet to the base. To enable persons of weak nerves to enjoy this somewhat exciting pleasure, a convenient railing has been attached to the rock, and clinging to this they can look down the dizzy height. Without this protection it would be wiser not to approach the edge of the rock at all. Glacier Point also forms a good standpoint whence to study the geological formation of the valley and the great mountain range to which it belongs. Situated at the point where the valley forks, the observer takes in at a glance the general outlines. Mirror Lake nestles at his feet, immediately in front is the grim and forbidding summit of Half Dome with his near neighbour, the Cap of Liberty, while to the right is the cañon named the Little Yosemite, through

From a photograph]   UPON GLACIER POINT.   *[by Taber, of San Francisco.*

which flows the Merced, which there forms two superb cataracts, the Nevada and the Vernal Falls. These nearer objects at first arrest attention, since in the clear atmosphere they appear quite close at hand, while in reality they are at considerable distances; but the eye soon begins to take

o

a wider sweep, and then gradually the observer realizes that he is in the very heart and centre of the vast Sierra Nevada. As far as vision can penetrate, north and south, stretch the lofty mountain peaks, solemn and stately, and ever covered with the white and glistening snow. That pointed crest that looks about four miles distant is Mount Lyell, an extinct volcano, 13,000 feet high, and twenty miles away as the crow flies. Those twin peaks that seem but a gunshot off are the Cathedral Towers, 8,000 feet high, and six miles distant. In both directions, rising one beyond another, stretch an apparently endless succession of these great mountains.

The ascent of Glacier Point is but one example of many similar mountain excursions afforded by this wonderful region. For the longer journeys to such peaks as Mount Lyell, it is needful to camp out, and also to incur a good deal of expense. And after all, the most impressive experience is the first sight of the valley itself. Not a few visitors enter it one day and leave it the next. But whether the stay be brief or lengthy, the mind is permanently enriched by pictures that will abide as long as life itself, and that often act as a refreshment in after days amid the cares and difficulties and sorrows and temptations of life. Amid the dingy commonplaces and arduous toils of so much of the daily round, the recollections of El Capitan, and Half Dome and Clouds' Rest, and the pleasant Merced flowing through the majestic valley, come as a refreshment to the weary mind, and as a new impulse to the flagging will.

If the state of the snow permits, it is pleasanter to enter the Yosemite by one route and leave it by another ; but at present this involves extra fatigue and longer stage journeys. Many prefer to return by the Raymond route, since they can thus visit the Mariposa Grove of Big Trees, the most accessible of the several forests of *Sequoia gigantea*, of which California is so proud. The start is from the Wawona Hotel in a stage of lighter construction than the one used to enter the Yosemite, but like that drawn by four horses. The road winds up through densely-wooded hills. The timber is magnificent, consisting chiefly of the sugar pine, Douglas spruce, and occasional oaks. Many of the pines might be mistaken for the Big Trees, as thousands of them attain a height of 150 or 200 feet, and measure five, six, or seven feet in diameter. After about an hour's ride, the first group of 'sequoias' is reached, and the first glance is sufficient to account for the popular name, Big Trees. The smallest of these forest giants are from eighteen to twenty feet in diameter, and tower aloft 200 or 300 feet into the sky. They grow in little patches or clusters, and are never found at lower elevations than 4,000 feet above the sea, or higher than 7,000 feet. They are clad in a reddish brown bark, deeply seamed, and about ten inches or a foot in thickness. The trunks are symmetrical, and rise from seventy-five to one hundred feet without a branch to break the grand outline. At that height a cluster of branches appears, and the stem is

THE GRIZZLY GIANT.

lined with them for one hundred or two hundred feet. The most unsatis-factory feature about these monsters is the abrupt way in which they end at the top. In proportion to their girth they ought to rise to a height of about five hundred feet; as it is they rarely exceed three hundred.

At the entrance to the grove stand two giants, named the Sentinels, and after passing them, others are descried at every few hundred feet. Each tree has received a name. Two which spring from a single root are known as Maryland and Virginia, others are named after famous men, as Lincoln and Grant.

One of the chief reasons for visiting this particular cluster, is to see what is commonly believed to be the largest tree on the continent, if not in the world. This magnificent specimen is known as the Grizzly Giant, and as he has weathered the storms and the changes of more than a thousand years, and begins to show signs of their wear and tear, he is appropriately described. A line passed round his bark at a level of six feet from the earth measures 102 feet, and a line passed through the tree at the same height would measure 33 feet. It is very hard to get a clear idea of what these figures mean; the average width of good class houses in London, say for example in Grosvenor Square or Piccadilly, is less than thirty-three feet. The trunk of this tree, if placed in front of one of these buildings would completely hide it. At a height of about eighty or one hundred feet above the ground, the first limb springs at right angles from the trunk, and at a distance of a few feet from the main stem takes a sharp bend upwards. This limb is six feet in diameter, that is, it equals in size most of the largest of the sugar pines. Although flourishing, in all probability, long before the time of the Roman Conquest of Britain, this patriarch gives many signs of vigorous health and seems likely to last for centuries to come.

The upper Mariposa Grove, some distance further through the forest, also contains a large number of these sylvan giants. The phenomenon of this part is the tree called Wawona, an Indian name which is said to signify 'big tree.' He has not rivalled the Grizzly Giant in size, but he has features of special interest peculiar to himself. In the lapse of centuries many of these big trees begin to decay at the base. The bark and the outer roots remain firm and sound, but the tree rots at the centre, and as the dead wood falls away, a hut or cavern is formed in the heart of the tree. Some of these are large enough to form a shelter for twelve to twenty persons, and to allow a horseman to ride in. Wawona is one of these, but the wood has been chopped away so as to make a tunnel right through the centre, and through this the waggon road passes. On the occasion of the writer's visit, his stage stopped in this tunnel; it carried eight persons, in addition to the driver, seated two by two behind each other, and the whole of the vehicle with the pair of near horses and the leaders as far as their shoulders, were all within the limits of the tree; the length through the tunnel being eight and twenty feet.

This variety of Big Tree grows only in California, and there only on the slopes of the Sierra Nevada. Its nearest relative, also limited to California, is the Red Wood, of which magnificent forests grow in the country just to the north of San Francisco. In size it is but little inferior to the *Sequoia.* Much of the timber used in San Francisco comes from the Red Wood forests.

The journey from San Francisco to Portland follows

another of the scenic railways of the west, called, after the great mountain of the same name, seen from so many points of view, the Shasta route. One of the loveliest spots on the journey is a little place called Mossbrae. The train stops beside a little Spa, and waits a few minutes while the passengers get out and drink the pure, strong soda water which is constantly bubbling up from the spring. The river runs down by the side of the railway, and the opposite bank rises very abruptly in the shape of a dome, down the face of which comes streaming over thick green moss, and through ferns, and amid lovely trees, a great number of little waterfalls which delight the eye with their beauty, and fill the ear with their pleasant ripple.

After leaving Mossbrae the railway climbs the mountains by a gradient of 175 feet to the mile, affording another fine example of loop engineering shown in the engraving on page 12. At one point the upper line is 600 feet directly above the lower, but in order to

MOSSBRAE.

reach that elevation the train has had to travel a distance of six or seven miles. After leaving McCloud the mountain Divide is crossed, and the first glimpses of the distant snow-clad peaks of Mount Shasta are obtained. The top and the upper slopes of the Divide are clothed with pine forests, which the railway has made it profitable to work, and consequently lumbering is going vigorously through all this region.

The train runs rapidly down the northern slope of the Divide until it reaches the station called Sissons. This place is the best starting-point for the ascent of Mount Shasta. This great mountain is the cone of a gigantic extinct volcano. It has three summits, the central and the highest rising 14,400 feet above the sea. The western summit, 12,000 feet high, is an enormous crater with a perfect rim. The plateau upon which Sissons stands is about 3,500 feet above the sea, and as no lower slopes intervene the eye ranges over a mountain slope 11,000 feet in height. The upper portion is clad in perpetual snowfields, pure and white, and gleaming in the sunshine; the mountain forms a superb natural marvel, once seen never to be forgotten. As you look up at the central peak standing out clearly and brilliantly against the sky, with the soft fleecy clouds resting here and there on the lower slopes, it is difficult to believe that the summit is just two miles in vertical height above the eye of the observer. For the next five or six hours the train slowly circles round the enormous mountain pile, and the towering peak is seen from many different points of view, and is equally lovely and equally impressive from them all. If a comparison must be made in point of beauty and impressiveness among the mountains of the world, Shasta, of which we give an engraving on page 12, must undoubtedly hold a high place in the front rank.

Just as the southern boundary of Oregon is reached, the railroad begins its second climb, this time across the Siskiyon Mountains. In the course of about twenty miles the road rises 2,000 feet, winding up a valley by the usual method of long loops. As the crown of the ridge is passed, a farewell glimpse of Shasta is caught in the far distance, and then the line runs through the fertile valleys of the Rogue and Willamette Rivers to Portland.

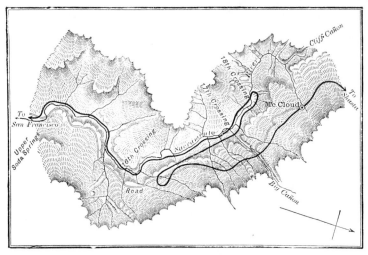

PLAN OF THE LOOP ON THE SHASTA RAILWAY, NEAR McCLOUD.

The Lower Falls and the Cañon of the Yellowstone from Point Lookout.

From a photograph]   THE HOT CONE IN THE YELLOWSTONE LAKE.   [*by Taber, of San Francisco.*

CHAPTER IX.

FROM PORTLAND TO THE YELLOWSTONE PARK.

THROUGH THE ROCKIES.

PORTLAND, the fast-growing commercial capital of the North-West, is situated on the Willamette River, about ten miles above its confluence with the Columbia, and about one hundred miles from the Pacific. It is a port, and vessels of all sizes and classes can reach its quays. The railway system of the North-West centres here, no less than six different lines having a terminus at Portland. Surrounded, too, by one of the richest farming districts in the world, Portland seems destined to a very great and powerful future. The growth in population has been very rapid, and has been largely helped by the development of the railway system. In 1880, the population was about 20,000 ; in 1890, it had increased to 70,000. The streets are well laid out, and, except in the heart of the business portion, they are lined with beautiful and comfortable homes surrounded by trees and flower gardens. The town is well supplied with public buildings, and the Portland Hotel is one of the largest, handsomest, and best furnished in the whole country. Signs of the most abundant prosperity abound on every hand, and the trade of the city, large as it already is, is increasing rapidly every year. The suburbs are very beautiful, and cable-cars convey visitors and residents easily and rapidly to these outlying districts. From Portland Heights splendid views are obtained over the valley of the Willamette, with the lofty snow-crowned peaks of the Cascade Mountains in the far distance.

Portland is a good starting-point for a trip up or down the Columbia River. The chief scenery lies between its junction with the Willamette River and a place called the Dalles, about one hundred miles above Portland. A good way to see this stretch of country is to go up the southern bank of the stream by the railway and then make the return journey by boat. At the Dalles the Columbia River forces its way through the Cascade Mountains, the great stream being compressed into a narrow channel lined with huge cliff walls which occasionally reach a height of 800 or 1,000 feet. About fifty miles below the Dalles are a series of rapids too sudden in their descent to be traversed by the steamer. Here a narrow-gauge railway, about five miles in length, makes a connection with the steamer which starts below the rapids. This portion of the river is one of the great centres of the salmon fishery, for which the Columbia is so famous. Nets are very little used, the chief method employed being fish-wheels. These are placed where the current is rapid, and are worked by the water. The construction is simple but very effective. A wheel about twenty-five feet in diameter, and eight feet wide, is placed in a large wooden frame so that it can be lowered to the depth of five or six feet into the current; or lifted, if need be, completely above its surface. It is divided into compartments like a paddle-wheel, only each compartment is made of a strong wire netting with large openings on the outer rim of the wheel. When lowered into the current the wheel begins to revolve in the direction of the stream, and as the salmon swim up the current they jump into the compartments of this wheel, and are instantly swung out of the water and fall into a trough so arranged around the axle of the wheel as to shoot the fish through an aperture at the side into a great tank prepared for their reception. It is most fascinating to watch one of these great wheels in action. Almost every turn brings up a fish, and sometimes half a dozen are flapping about in the compartments of the wheel at the same moment. Three or four, ranging from fifteen to fifty pounds in weight, will be caught in a single revolution. The season is from April till July; and about five tons of salmon are caught every twenty-four hours in one of these wheels. The law compels all wheels to be lifted from the water from 6 P.M. on Saturday till 6 P.M. Sunday.

A few miles below the cascades is a large salmon-canning establishment. It stands on the banks of the river, partly overhanging it, and consists of three storeys, one on the level of the water where the fish are received, the middle one in which the chief work of the establishment is done, and an upper floor on which the cans are manufactured. The fish are brought in from the wheels by steam launches, large quantities of them being floated

A Salmon Wheel on the Columbia River.

down the stream from the wheels and picked up by the launches as they come abreast of the factory. The salmon are immediately cleaned and scaled, the refuse being thrown into the stream. Chinamen do all the work, and the sight of them and the methods they employ is not appetizing. Division of labour is in full force, and the fish under operation of this law is rapidly passed from hand to hand. He is placed upon a great knife—consisting of seven curved blades, if he be large, and three or four, if small—worked by a powerful handle, and is immediately divided into small equal sections. These are swept on to men who cut them up into smaller pieces with large hand-knives. Then the fragments pass to another set, who cram them tightly into the cans with their hands, and then they are soldered down by machinery, and passed on by running bands to the great ovens where they are steamed for three quarters of an hour. The liquid which is formed in the tins is then driven out, through a tiny vent left in the can for the purpose, by hammering the tin; it is re-soldered and marked, and is then ready for packing. So expeditious is the method, that a fifty-pound salmon swimming at his ease in the Columbia at 9 A.M. may be on his way, in bright new tins, to some remote quarter of the globe by 6 P.M.

From Harper's Magazine.　　　Copyright, by Harper & Brothers.

CAPE HORN, ON THE COLUMBIA RIVER.

The scenery of the Lower Columbia is often very highly praised, and is certainly remarkable for the rich colouring and the bold forms of many of the cliffs; but it is somewhat of an exaggeration to describe it as far surpassing in beauty the Rhine or the Hudson. Cape Horn, of which we give an engraving, is one of the most noted spots. During the descent of the river, very fine views are obtained of the snowy summit of Mount Hood. This portion of the Cascade Mountains is very rich in great peaks, notably Mount Hood, Mount Adams, and Mount Tacoma; their lofty snow-clad summits may often be seen upon the sky-line sixty or eighty miles away.

Portland has a young and vigorous rival one hundred miles away to the north called Tacoma; and a few miles further north still, situated like Tacoma on the shore of Puget Sound, is the town of Seattle. Both are growing with a speed unrivalled elsewhere in the world, and the inhabitants of Tacoma are inclined to the view that it will in the near future surpass

MOUNT TACOMA.

San Francisco and Portland in power and commercial importance, and become the great Pacific port of the United States.

At Tacoma begins the eastward journey to St. Paul, nearly 2,000 miles away, along the trunk line of the Northern Pacific, the youngest of the three great routes from the Mississippi to the Pacific. Just before crossing the eastern boundary of the State of Washington, the town of Spokane Falls is reached. This is one of the best illustrations in the United States of the rapid way in which natural advantages develop towns when they are made accessible by the railroad. At this point the Spokane River by a series of cascades descends 150 feet in the course of half a mile, thus providing an immense amount of water-power. This was useless for all practical purposes until the Northern Pacific passed through the town. Only ten or twelve years ago it was open country, with hardly a house or a family in the neighbourhood; now the rapids are lined with saw mills, flour mills, printing offices, and electric generators, a large town has sprung up with hotels, and fine business premises, electric tramways and many of the conveniences of ordinary civilisation. Already the usual fire has swept away many of the original wooden houses, and their sites are being occupied by stone and brick buildings. Everything is yet in the rough, the inhabitants not having had time to pave the wide and regular streets, and few of the wooden houses are so much as painted. But it is within the bounds of possibility, and even probability, that in the year 2000 Spokane Falls will be a large and flourishing city of 50,000 or 100,000 inhabitants.

After leaving Spokane Falls the Northern Pacific traverses the States of Idaho and Montana, on its way to St. Paul. Montana is one of the chief ranch and cattle-raising districts; in it also is Livingston, the junction for the side excursion to the Yellowstone Park. To this place we shall return immediately after a few words upon the main journey. In the proper season, both in Colorado and Montana, large herds of cattle being driven to a 'round-up' are often in full view from the car windows. The 'round-up' is a term applied to the gathering together of the vast numbers of cattle, scattered over a wide district of country, which have been feeding on the plains for months, and are collected at the appointed time and place by the cowboys in order that the calves may all be branded with the mark of their proper owner. One of the most difficult parts of this duty is to 'cut out' a beast from the particular herd in which it is found. This is done by riding into the herd upon a carefully-trained horse or pony, and skilfully separating the beast from its companions. As soon as the animals wanted from a herd have been 'cut out,' the rest are driven away; those that are left are then branded, an operation which always means hard work and very often considerable danger. This part of a ranchman's life is both toilsome and exciting, but seems to be enjoyed by those who take part in it.

Montana is also a great horse-raising district, and here the 'bronco-buster,' whose work is to break into the saddle perfectly wild horses, finds plenty of occupation. This is done in a rough-and-ready manner, two or three rides of an hour or two each on successive days being considered quite sufficient, and five or ten dollars being the usual fee. A first-class rider of this kind usually receives pretty high wages, which he richly deserves, for his occupation, like that of the man who carries the dynamite charges through the oil country, is one not likely to allow him to grow old.

After leaving Montana the line continues on its way running in a nearly straight line across North Dakota, one of the chief grain districts of the world, rich prairie land as flat as a pancake, and then in a south-easterly direction through Minnesota. Things are taken leisurely, and if a freight train gets off the line, or if an engine breaks down, the passengers wander around enjoying the scenery, gathering the wild flowers, or chafing helplessly at the delay. At length Minneapolis is reached, the great centre of the western trade in grain, the rival and young competitor of St. Paul. At this town, the capital of the State of Minnesota, situated upon the Mississippi nearly 2,000 miles from its mouth, the inexorable limits of space compel us to bring our wanderings amid the great cities and the glorious scenery of the great Republic to a close. But before doing this we must pay a brief visit to the far-famed Yellowstone National Park.

At Livingston, a growing little town nearly 900 miles from

A 'Bronco-Buster' Riding a Bucking Horse.

Portland on the west, and 1,030 miles from St. Paul on the east, a branch line runs due south a distance of fifty-one miles to Cinnabar, the starting-point for the Yellowstone National Park, the wonderland of the United States, with a very good claim to be considered the wonderland of the world. It

P

occupies the north-western corner of the State of Wyoming, and is sixty-five miles in length from north to south, and fifty-five miles from east to west, thus covering an area of 3,575 square miles. In this centre the great Rocky Mountain chain reaches its culminating point in a cluster of peaks and mountain ranges, which enclose a unique lake basin; and here the three longest rivers in the United States—the Missouri, the Columbia and the Colorado—take their rise. No portion of the Park lies at a lower elevation than 6,000 feet above the sea, and many parts are so much higher that the mean elevation of the whole plateau is about 8,000 feet. Yellowstone Lake, a most lovely sheet of water twenty-two miles long, and from

THE FALLS OF ST. ANTHONY AT ST. PAUL.

ten to fifteen miles wide, is 7,788 feet above the sea, and is shut in on almost every side by lofty peaks that rise another 3,000 or 5,000 feet. It is difficult to realise that the surface of the water in this lake is nearly 2,000 feet higher than the top of the loftiest mountain in Great Britain.

There is no doubt that the formation of this district is due to violent volcanic action in the distant past. Dr. Hayden, to whom the Government entrusted the direction of the first scientific survey of the Park, says: 'It is probable that during the Pliocene period the entire country drained by the sources of the Yellowstone and the Columbia was the scene of volcanic activity as great as that of any portion of the globe. It might be called one vast crater, made up of a thousand smaller volcanic vents and fissures, out of which the fluid interior of the earth, fragments of rock, and volcanic dust were poured in unlimited quantities. Hundreds of the cones of these

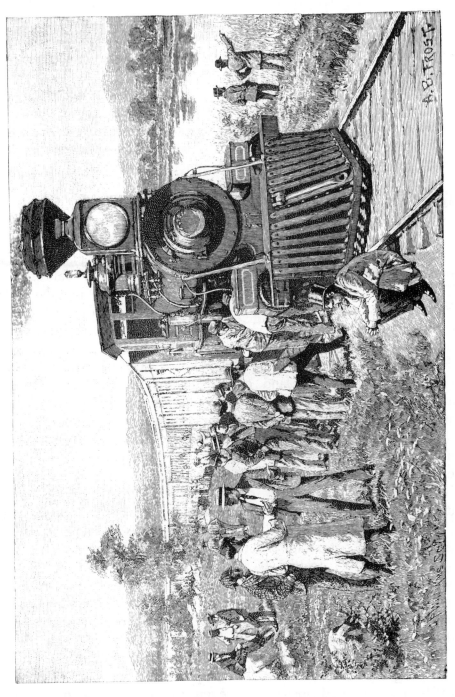

A BREAKDOWN ON THE LINE.

volcanic vents are now remaining, some of them rising to a height of 10,000 to 11,000 feet above the sea. Mounts Longford, Stevenson, Holmes, and more than a hundred other peaks may be seen from any high peak on any side of the basin, each of which formed a centre of effusion.'

It is a surprising fact that until the year 1870 the marvels of this district were unknown to all but a few stray trappers and Indians. A few of these had spread rumours of the wonders they had witnessed, and in August 1870, a party of officials and leading citizens of Montana, under the command of General Washburn and Lieutenant Doane, traversed the valley of the Yellowstone River, explored the Great Cañon, stood on the shores of Yellowstone Lake, and visited the great geysers of the Firehole River. They returned convinced that they had seen, to use their own words, 'the greatest wonders on the continent, and that there was not on the globe another region where, within the same limits, Nature had crowded so much of grandeur and majesty with so much of novelty and wonder.'

The report of their discovery led to the organisation, in 1871, of a large scientific expedition in combination with a survey made by officers in the United States Army. The result of this exploration was to make the marvels of the district widely known; and in the spring of 1872, Congress determined to reserve the whole district as a park for national use.

The great natural features of the Yellowstone Park are the Mammoth Hot Springs, the Lower and the Upper Geyser Basins, the Yellowstone Lake, and the Falls and the Grand Cañon of the Yellowstone River. But the comparatively trivial things in this wonderland are almost as remarkable as the phenomena which act on the great scale. The Park is rich in landscapes of great beauty, and is a land of streams and waterfalls, and vale and mountain. Here too the buffalo has found at last a secure resting-place, and here he is carefully preserved by Government authority. Here too the jaded traveller is occasionally stimulated by the sight of a bear, to say nothing of manifold varieties of smaller game. He is charmed by the sight of the soft fleecy cloud which lingers on the near mountain top; but he is surprised as he draws nearer to discover that it proceeds out of the mountain, and instead of fleecy cloud is composed of hot steam. He sees what appears to be a clear babbling brook by the wayside, yet is somewhat startled when he notices that the ripples in its course are due, not to the pebbles in its bed, but to the fact that the water is boiling. He hears a sound in the grassy field which borders the road, and on seeking its cause, he finds a hollow in the earth from which come hoarse rumblings and sounds of violent subterranean action. He sees a pool apparently presenting nothing but the calm surface of still water; but on reaching the brink and looking into the clear depths he sees a vision of beauty in form and in colour far beyond the power of any artist or sculptor to reproduce. In some parts the rocks assume weird forms, and even the trees have turned to stone. And as he passes day after day amid these varied and abnormal sights and sounds, he reaches a state of mind in which he ceases to be surprised at any departure from the ordinary course of Nature in the sights under his eye and the sounds in his ears.

By the route usually followed, the Park is entered at the northern extremity and along the valley of the Gardiner River. Here are found the Mammoth Hot Springs, and here is the great hotel from which the various staging excursions start. The hotel stands upon a terrace which, though no longer the scene of volcanic action, shows many traces of its presence in the past; the chief being the cone of an extinct geyser known as the Cap of Liberty, fifty-two feet high and twenty feet in diameter, built up by layers of deposit from the water which in former days used to flow through the opening at the top. From this level rises up Terrace Mountain, itself an outlying spur of the larger and higher White Mountain beyond it. This has been built up by the action of boiling water slowly bubbling up from many springs and forming the terraces by their overflow.

Seen from the front the appearance is that of a hill about 150 feet to 200 feet high, the face of it broken up into a series of wide terraces which rise one above another. Each of these terraces contains a number of springs separated from one another by little ridges of deposit, beautiful in form and often exquisitely coloured. The water trickles slowly over the face of the terrace, at first giving the impression that what the eye sees is a waterfall; a closer inspection reveals the fact that the apparent fall is mineral matter which has solidified into beautiful shapes of falling water. Wherever the spring has ceased to flow, the colouring is nearly always a creamy white; but here, as elsewhere in Nature, the cessation of life is the signal for decay. A terrace no longer moistened by the water begins to crumble and lose its faultless beauty of form. Wherever the water is still running, whether continuously or at intervals, the formation is sharp and distinct, and the colouring rich and varied. Some of the terraces are a pinkish white, deepening almost to a crimson. Many of them are a rich terra-cotta shading off into various tints of brown; others are verging on yellow with various shades of pearl grey passing to the purest white. This formation extends over a space of from half a mile to a mile in width, and from fifty to two hundred feet in height, and seen under a clear sky in the brilliant sunshine is marvellous for its beauty both of form and tone.

The terraces can be climbed, and upon reaching the top of the largest it is seen to contain a level area from half a mile to a mile square. The first impression is a bewildering mass of blended colour; the whole area seems paved with mosaics arranged in red and blue and white and brown and golden circles. It is easy with care to walk out upon this lovely pavement, and then a careful scrutiny reveals the secret of its composition. It is made up of a series of circular springs, the rim being firm and solid, the centre in a great majority of cases gently bubbling up from the interior of the mountain. The colour lies for the most part around the inner circumference of the ring, the portion nearest to the outer wall very often looking like the whitest porcelain, and immediately within this lies the band of strong colour, pink, brown, yellow, or a vivid blue. Through the centre the eye can sometimes see deeply into the clear water. The whole mountain has been built up by this slow steady overflow of the water depositing rapidly the solid matter it holds in solution.

Some of the smaller terraces on the lower slopes have received fancy names—the chief being Minerva Terrace, forty feet high, with an area of nearly an acre; and Jupiter Terrace, containing a spring one hundred feet in diameter, and covering an area of about five acres. The water in the springs of the Park contains large quantities of silica in solution, and as

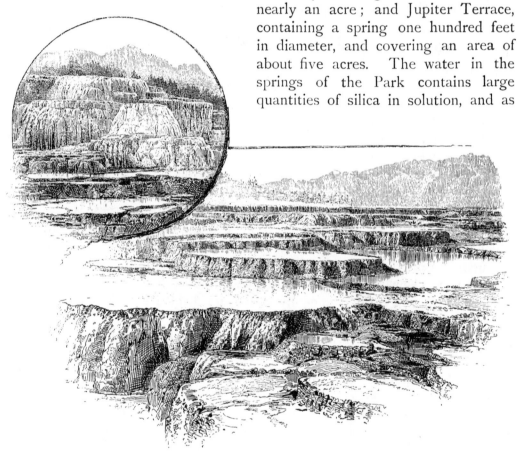

From photographs]   THE MAMMOTH HOT SPRINGS.   *[by Haynes, of St. Paul.*

it has cooled and evaporated, this silica has made up the bulk of the hard, white substance which now covers many square miles of the valley, and is everywhere spoken of as the 'formation;' but the water of the Mammoth Hot Springs contains a very large amount of carbonate of lime, and of this substance the bulk of the terraces which we have just described is composed. The richer veins of colour are due to the sulphur, iron, alum, and other materials found in the waters.

After leaving the Mammoth Hot Springs, the route through the Park follows a road to the south, which passes through the Golden Gate, a rugged mountain road clinging to the side of a hill called Bunsen's Peak. By this means access is gained to a plateau 1,000 feet higher than the level of the springs, and for some miles many of the great peaks of the Gallatin Mountains are in full view. The road then runs between Beaver Lake and a great cliff, which the driver informs his passengers is composed entirely of black glass. It is really a mass of obsidian, a kind of mineral glass, jet black, the result of volcanic action, and, when any of the masses which fall from this cliff have been broken and expose a recent surface to the air, they present a

From a photograph]   THE OBSIDIAN CLIFF.   *[by Haynes, of St. Paul.*

glistening, mirror-like appearance in the sunshine. In earlier times this cliff was a neutral ground to the various tribes of Rocky Mountain Indians, the material being much more suitable in their judgment for arrow-heads than flint, the ordinary material in everyday use.

The next stopping-place is the Norris Geyser Basin, and here the first considerable evidences of geyser action manifest themselves. The basin covers an area of six square miles, and presents an appearance that can only be adequately described as infernal. The 'formation' is a large, nearly level basin, generally white in colour, but enlivened here and there with patches of brown and blue and green. The prevalent odour is decidedly sulphurous, and from all parts of the broad expanse jets of steam are incessantly issuing, while here and there tiny geysers leap up at frequent intervals into the air. Close by the road is the Steam Vent, a hole from whence night and day there issues a roaring column of steam, like that of a powerful engine fretting to get to work. Only twenty or thirty feet away is a circular stone cauldron about ten feet in diameter, filled with water which incessantly boils, leaping up angrily in constant spurts to a height of three or four feet. In some respects this is the most uncanny object in the Park, as the water boils with a vehemence peculiar to itself. A short distance beyond this witches' cauldron, from a concealed hole in a steep bank, there issues a continuous succession of hollow rumbles, as though in the depths of the earth demons were playing bowls. This phenomenon has been named the Black Growler. Continuing the journey we come to a pool of dirty, slate-coloured water.

'A MINUTE MAN.'
(From a photograph by Haynes, of St. Paul.)

The surface is perfectly still, and lies from two to three feet below the edge of the rocky reservoir; but even as you watch, the water begins to sway, then to bubble and to rise, and finally leaps eight or ten feet into the air, giving off a cloud of steam, and then sinks down again into silence and quiescence. This performance occurs at regular intervals of fourteen minutes. In the same neighbourhood are a number of 'minute men,' that is, tiny geysers which go off at sixty seconds, and which are exceedingly interesting from the prompt regularity with which they act. The subterranean forces are always active in this basin, and new geysers, some of them of very large size, are constantly forcing their way to the surface.

It takes some little time to enjoy any lengthy stay in this region; the impression made is altogether too accurately described by the phrase 'living on the edge of a volcano.' As you step upon the hard, white 'formation' to inspect more closely some one of its many marvels, you hear, or think you hear, an ominous echo of your footstep, which gives you the impression that you tread upon a thin crust, liable at any moment to give way, and let you through to certain destruction in the boiling depths below.

The next stage in the journey is the Lower Geyser Basin, twenty miles distant. This is a plateau 7,250 feet above the sea, containing about seven hundred hot springs and seventeen geysers. The road to the basin passes through the Gibbon Cañon, and at one point there are some very picturesque falls. It then crosses a high ridge covered with pine and fir trees, and just as the descent on the southern side is commenced, upon a clear day, the three giant peaks of the Teton Mountains, shown in the engraving on page 9 can be distinctly seen, although they are seventy-five miles away.

The hotel is not well situated as regards beauty of surroundings, and in its general equipment in 1890 reflected anything but credit upon the United States Government. Whenever there is a pressure upon the accommodation this proves to be totally inadequate. Although Congress has reserved the Park for public use, it considers the question of the public convenience far too trivial a matter upon which to expend either thought or money. And so it farms out the hotel arrangements to speculators whose sole object is to make money. It is true that United States officers are on the spot, and exceedingly courteous and obliging the writer found them; but in any matter relating to the hotels they are, or at any rate they appear to be, powerless. The attendance, the rooms and the general management at the Norris, and Lower and Upper Geyser Basin hotels in the year 1890 were little short of scandalous. An American gentleman's remark on leaving the Park puts the case pithily and truly, so far as the writer's experience goes. Said he, 'When I look on the beauties and wonders of this region, I am proud of my country; when I think of the disgusting inconveniences we have suffered, all of which could be prevented by a little official care, I am ashamed of my Government.' It is certainly a good thing for Congress to reserve the Park for public use; it would be not only the logical sequence, but also a graceful completion to its work, if it insisted that the pleasure of the travellers, whom by the very act of con-stituting it a National Park, Congress invites as visitors, was not diminished by a temporary but compulsory lapse into semi-barbarism.

The most remarkable objects to be studied at the Lower Basin are the Fountain Geyser and the Mammoth Paint Pots. The former has a crater about thirty feet in diameter, and when in action the water is frequently thrown up to a height of fifty or sixty feet. On approaching it only an irregular circle of brownish white geyserite, as the substance deposited by the continuous overflow of the water is called, can be seen. But when near enough to look into the water, an involuntary exclamation of delight rises to the lips. The water is so marvellously clear, that for some moments the great depth of the crater is not realized. The water is enclosed within sides irregular in shape, with rounded bosses, and ledges and little caverns, all exquisite in form. At the surface the colouring of the walls is white, and then, as the water deepens, passes by the most delicate gradations through greenish hues into a superb turquoise tint. The eye can see no bottom, and the dark centre suggestive of fathomless depth conveys a weird impression that heightens the fascination exercised by the subtle beauty of the sides. These are so lovely that the observer would fain examine them more closely ; but their beauty seems a lure to drag him to the grim and hopeless depths beneath.

The Mammoth Paint Pots are a splendid example of another class of hot springs. In some parts the geysers throw up mud instead of water, occasionally sending up jets thirty to fifty feet high. But this remarkable mud cauldron is about sixty feet long, and forty feet wide, and is surrounded by a rim from four to five feet in height. The whole of this basin is filled with a mass of fine pinky-white silicious clay ; through this mass steam is incessantly bubbling, with just sufficient force to cause the clay to assume the most lovely rose forms. As one cluster disappears another appears. In some parts the clay rises in cones and rings and jets. It bears a very close resemblance to paint, and hence the name. Part of the surface is broken up into smaller circles, and in these the steam acts with sufficient force to cause little pellets to be shot from side to side of the circle, a tiny explosion following the discharge of each morsel ; the impression being that a company of little hobgoblins are at play, and pelting each other with globules of the clay.

On leaving this district the road follows the course of the Firehole River, traversing a part known by the suggestive name of Hell's Half Acre. Here are more springs with most lovely colouring, and here also is the huge Excelsior Geyser, very irregular in action, but when in full swing by far the largest and most violent in the whole Park.

The Upper Geyser Basin is, however, by far the most popular, and is likely to remain so ; for the simple reason that here, into a very limited area, are crowded many of the largest and most extraordinary geysers, and that hardly an hour passes without an eruption. The basin occupies about four square miles, but the chief geysers are concentrated into about one square mile. Through the centre of the basin flows the Firehole River, and along the course of this stream the chief manifestations of volcanic force appear. On all sides are mountain slopes covered with dark pine trees. Clouds of steam hang over the whole of the area, and in whatever direction the eye turns, graceful spiral columns of it are seen ascending. The dark amphitheatre of pine trees forms a splendid background, and heightens the effect of the ceaseless clouds of steam, and the many terrific exhibitions of geyser power.

The first visited by nearly every traveller is the Old Faithful Geyser. This is because the hotel at which the stages stop is only a few hundred yards away, and however irregular the action of his great brothers and sisters may be, he himself is always 'on time.' At intervals of every sixty-three minutes, day and night, the amazing phenomenon of his eruption occurs. As you walk towards the cone, five minutes before the appointed time, you see a low, gently sloping mound of geyserite, and even when you look into the crater you can see only an irregular opening in the surface.

From a photograph]   THE CASTLE GEYSER IN ACTION.   *[by Haynes, of St. Paul.*

But, as you watch, the water begins to shoot up a few spasmodic jets, and then suddenly a column of hot water about two feet in diameter rises from 125 feet to 150 feet, and continues playing in the form of an exquisitely beautiful fountain for nearly five minutes. The frontispiece gives some faint notion of the scene. Great clouds of steam escape from the rising and falling water during the whole eruption. When a breeze is blowing it is possible to stand on the windward side, even while the geyser is in active discharge, within a few feet of the rushing stream. Some of the water flows down the leeward side of the cone, but the bulk returns to the reservoir whence it came. The most remarkable feature about this geyser is the regularity and punctuality of its action. Upon one occasion when the writer was 'on time' for an afternoon display, the geyser was several minutes late ; and a guide, who happened to be standing near, remarked 'that Old Faithful was sometimes a trifle lazy after lunch !'

The cone of Old Faithful is a good position from whence to gain an idea of the relative situation of the different geysers. There are at least twenty-six of these, and about five hundred hot springs in the basin. In the near foreground of the opposite bank of the river are the Beehive Geyser —so called from the shape of the cone—the Giantess, which only acts about once a fortnight, but then lasts for nearly twelve hours, the Lion, Lioness, and Cubs, and a large number of smaller geysers. On the left bank of the stream in the near foreground is the Castle Geyser, so called from the shape of its cone ; and in the distance are the Grand, the Giant, the Splendid, and the Grotto. It is impossible to attempt a description of each of these marvels, and so we give sketches and engravings of the Castle and the Splendid in action, and these may be taken, other things being equal, as good representatives of them all.

The Castle Geyser occupies the most prominent position in the basin, the cone being unusually large. It has a diameter at the base of more than one hundred feet, and is twenty or thirty feet high. The opening at the top is circular in shape, about three feet in diameter, and of a bright orange colour. In accordance with his dignity the Castle usually gives ample notice of an eruption. This occurs about every thirty hours, and for five or six hours prior to the great event, jets of water are thrown up from fifteen to twenty feet. During the eruption proper a column of water shoots up into the air seventy-five to one hundred feet, and continues to play for about half-an-hour. Then follows an escape of steam, which makes a hoarse roaring, audible for a long distance, and lasting about the same time as the boiling fountain. On the north side of the cone is a hot spring, formerly a favourite resort of campers, where excellent coffee can be boiled in fifteen minutes, and where Nature has kindly provided a kitchen-range for cooking.

The Splendid Geyser is more capricious, and is in many respects one of the most remarkable in the whole valley. It has no cone, the crater being almost on the same level as the surrounding expanse of 'formation.' It condescends to act only every other day, but upon that day it supplies an eruption every three hours. We planned to witness one due soon after 3 P.M., and arrived about 3.15. Looking into the crater we could see the water just a trifle agitated, and it was much too hot to touch. About 3.30 a delicate, exquisitely-formed cone of white hot water shot up about ten

THE CRATER OF THE SPLENDID GEYSER.

feet, and then, just as it was falling back into the crater, came a rush and a sound of violent hissing, and then a cone of water and steam lovely in form, and gleaming like diamond in the sunshine, sprang up to a height of eighty or one hundred feet. This continued to play for some five minutes. At intervals of a few seconds a jet would shoot twenty or thirty feet higher than the main mass, and then fall back upon it in a shower of the loveliest spray. All fortunate enough to witness this display agree that the geyser well deserves its name.

From the Upper Geyser Basin there are two main routes to the Grand Cañon; one is to retrace the journey as far as the Norris

THE SPLENDID GEYSER IN ACTION.
(*From a photograph by Haynes, of St. Paul.*)

Geyser Basin, and then proceed in an easterly direction. The other, and by far the most enjoyable, skirts the southern shore of Shoshone Lake, crosses the Continental Divide, skirts the north-western shores of the Yellowstone Lake, and then follows the left bank of the Yellowstone River, passing the Great Mud Geyser, traversing the lovely Hayden Valley, and finally reaching the Grand Cañon Hotel. In the Yellowstone Lake, at a point not far from the shore, is the oft-referred-to Hot Cone. Standing upon this the fisherman can secure his trout in the lake, and then, without removing it from the hook, cook it in the boiling water.

Wonderful the geysers undoubtedly are, and lovely in form and colour many of the hot springs; but if a choice had to be made the majority would probably place the Grand Cañon of the Yellowstone not only at the head of the wonders of the Park, but as probably the most marvellous exhibition of Nature's handiwork on the whole continent. After a careful study of the whole district the conviction is reached that this pre-eminence is due to the concentration here of many beauties, each of which may be seen separately in as remarkable a form elsewhere. The Grand Cañon of the Colorado is on a much more magnificent scale, but none of its walls compare with these in richness and variety of colouring. More water passes over Niagara in a week, probably, than flows through the Cañon in a year, and yet there is nothing at Niagara that approaches the Lower Fall of the Yellowstone in picturesque beauty. The scenery of the Yosemite is on a much more imposing scale, and the waterfalls in that region can perhaps compete most successfully with those of the Yellowstone; but the prevailing cold grey tints of the Yosemite granite compare but feebly with the glorious warmth of colour spread so richly over the miles of precipitous slope which here ravish the sight.

The Yellowstone River is the outlet of the lake of the same name, and after a course of hundreds of miles the waters swell the stream of the Missouri. About eighteen miles below the lake, after a peaceful career through pleasant open country, the river suddenly breaks into a rapid and then quickly reaches the Upper Falls. There the water takes a perpendicular leap of about 140 feet, and then flows swiftly for less than a mile until it reaches the Lower Fall. Here the river, although some 150 feet wide higher up the stream, narrows to about 75 feet, and the water plunges down for 360 feet, and then winds rapidly by a serpentine course through several miles of cañon. It is immediately below the Great Fall that the culminating point of beauty is reached. The great rocky walls wind in and out along the tortuous course of the stream, and slope so abruptly that the real bank of the river is the top of the cliff, which in many parts is 1,000 or 1,200 feet above the rushing water. This winding formation prevents the possibility of any one view embracing the whole cañon; but at several points it can be seen for the space of two or three miles. The most easily accessible is

Look-out Point, a projection of the rocky wall about 1,000 feet above the river, with the Lower Falls in full view on the right, and the cañon winding away to the left. Gazing upon this scene of surpassing beauty one realizes why the river has obtained its name. Various shades of yellow run through these rocky walls like a dominant tone, and superimposed on this are rich masses of vivid bold colouring which blend into a most superb painting from Nature's hand. Here the eye rests upon a mass of deep blood red, and there the whole wall is covered with many shades of pink and grey and pearly white; while below all, and binding all into one lovely landscape, runs the river like a band of living green, except where it is lashed into the purest white by the rocks and boulders which obstruct its current.

Once seen, this view from either Look-out or Inspiration Point has permanently enriched and enlarged the mental conception. No one can have imagined such a picture of supreme loveliness; no one having rejoiced in its beauty can ever lose its memory. It abides, like the influence of some deep spiritual emotion or like the clasp of a loved hand. And the more it is visited, and the more familiar its lineaments, the more it seems to baffle any attempt adequately to describe it. Age after age this has been a poem in stone and colour, seen only by an occasional wandering Indian, and by Him part of whose earthly robe of beauty it is. Indifferent indeed to all higher than sensuous claims must he be who can look upon this outward expression of Divine loveliness and not lift the heart in grateful thankfulness. 'Marvellous are thy works, O Lord; in wisdom hast Thou made them all.' As the writer gazed upon the vivid and manifold glories scattered in such rich abundance here the mind asked, 'To what *can* this be compared?' And the answer came in the thought, 'Only to one of the richest and most gorgeous of Norwegian sunsets by sudden petrifaction transformed into these rocky walls.'

THE LENOX LIBRARY, NEW YORK.

INDEX.